THE COUNTRY BAKEHOUSE

Traditional Baking
from the Country Kitchen

CHRISTOPHER CONIL

The Crowood Press

First published in 1988 by
The Crowood Press
Ramsbury, Marlborough
Wiltshire SN8 2HE

British Library Cataloguing in Publication Data

Conil, Christopher
  The country bakehouse.
  1. Baking
  I. Title
  641.7'1   TX765

ISBN 1 85223 081 9

Dedicated to Suzanne, Phillip, Matthew and Nicola

Acknowledgements

Marriage and Son Ltd, Chelmsford, Essex for their support and use of their test kitchen.
Camy Maertens for his enthusiasm and contribution to this book.
Suzanne, my wife, whose endearing loyalty and scrutiny over each recipe will be remembered long after the final print.
Jean Conil, my father, whose many books on French and Continental cookery have been my inspiration.
To those craftsmen who have left their mark in the recipe books of the world.

Photography by Stonecastle Graphics
Line illustrations by Pat Warren
Cover design by Vic Giolitto

Typeset by Grassroots, London N3
Printed in Great Britain by
Billing and Sons Ltd, Worcester

Contents

Introduction

Traditional cooking and baking has, over the past few years, enjoyed a dramatic and long overdue revival. The return to home baking using more natural ingredients has gone hand-in-hand with a desire to recapture the romance of days long past. This book, *The Country Bakehouse*, is a nostalgic look back to the days when the kitchen was the heart of the home and depended on the crops and produce of the surrounding land. We can't turn the clock back but we can still revel in the thought that home baking is exciting and fun to do and that there is nothing to compare with the fragrant aromas of freshly baked bread straight from the oven!

It gives me special pleasure to present this collection of traditional recipes and ideas. Cooking in general, and baking in particular, has played an enormous part in my life. When I was nine I followed my father around many well known restaurants and hotels. I was forever being shuttled from one kitchen to another, watching, observing closely and sometimes tasting the creations (or catastrophes) of the new vogue chefs and pâtissiers who were emerging in the 1950s. Waiting in the wing for theatrical culinary presentations was always very exciting. The height of the chefs' hats meant nothing to me — the star was always 'The Dish'. The hustle and bustle and care and attention revolved around 'The Dish'. The waiting client never knew just how much effort went into those little edible masterpieces. Surrounded by such cuisine, it was no wonder that my taste for the good life developed. Having an internationally famous French chef, Jean Conil, as a father and a successful Irish SRN as a mother, my childhood was happy and took on a cosmopolitan air. Living in Britain made no difference. I understood that one did not alter traditions, even in the kitchen. I can remember my father exploding — sometimes his French got in the way — at the English commis chefs and waiters who adopted the principle 'If they don't complain, it must be all right!'

I came to realise that a technical training was essential for success and yet a great deal was learnt just by watching. I quickly decided that a little doing would help too, and I have been employing the resulting treasured skills ever since.

In the course of my travels in search of inspiration I am constantly bombarded with new, technical ideas from the boffins who try to persuade us to try their latest kitchen gadgets, and indeed, where would we be without all these labour-saving devices? But I constantly return to the traditional kitchen crafts of my upbringing, when the most important thing was providing nourishment and sustenance to the family, using simple methods and natural farm produce. It is to these I return now in *The Country Bakehouse*. Of course I have adopted many of today's remarkable kitchen aids, including the microwave, but I hope very much that the spirit of the recipes is rooted firmly in the best traditions of our rural past and that it is this spirit which is recreated each time the bakehouse door is opened.

With this in mind, I have attempted to use only the best of ingredients — those which are naturally grown, or, in the case of animal produce, those which are produced by traditional methods of farming. Whilst it is prudent to consider the implications of 'too much of a good thing,' my simple philosophy is to eat enough which is enjoyable and nutritionally beneficial to you and not to become too obsessive about every calorie eaten. The body can be very resilient and, like a car, it burns fuel continually. Providing it is serviced regularly, it will last many years!

In the following eight chapters I have compiled and created a mixture of recipes which I hope will stimulate the avid home baker. I have kept to the traditions we hold dear and have only broken those which can be improved. If you love baking and can use naturally produced ingredients wherever possible, you too can relive the moments when an affectionate, warm smile welcomed family and friends to your Country Bakehouse!

Christopher Conil
Master Baker

Notes on Ingredients and Equipment

INGREDIENTS

The finished, baked, article will be determined by three important factors — correct weighing, method or technique and skill in preparation and choice of ingredients, which should always be the very best quality you can buy. For a list of the terms used in the recipe instructions, see the Glossary.

Flours

100% Wholemeal: Wholemeal flour is the whole grain ground to a coarse or fine flour meal. The two milling methods used today are Roller-milled and Stone-milled. Both produce an excellent flour. The Roller-milled type tends to be finer than the Stone-milled type, which is milled in very much the same way as in years gone by. Wholemeal is high in fibre and very nutritious. All the recipes in this book can be made with wholemeal flour — just substitute it for the white flour where mentioned and adjust the water to ensure you achieve a smooth elastic dough. Wholemeal flour tends to absorb more water than white, so this is an important point to note.

Wheatmeal: This is a brown flour which is more refined than 100% Wholemeal (some 85—90% of the wheat is used in wheatmeal flour). It produces bread and cakes of a lighter texture.

Malted flour (granary-type): This flour is now available at most supermarkets and contains malted wheat grains — those bits which tend to stick to your teeth. Bread made with this flour tends to have a delicious nutty, malted flavour which is very tasty toasted.

Germ-meal (Hovis): Wheatgerm is added together with salt to brown flour and gives a unique flavour. It is full of goodness being the heart of the grain.

Rye flour: This is darker in colour with a strong 'rustic' flavour. It is also low in gluten, which makes it softer. When breadmaking, use half rye and half strong white flour for rye breads.

Strong white flour (breadmaking flour): This is flour with a high gluten content and is suitable for bread, puff and Danish pastry and various fruit cakes. In this book use strong flour (or any of the brown flours) for all the bread recipes.

Also available now is organically-grown untreated flour which appears creamy in colour but produces very good bread and pastries.

Soft (plain) flour: This is lower in gluten and therefore suitable for cakes, short pastry, biscuits and puddings. A little added cornflour will improve the texture of flour confectionery.

Cornmeal: This is made from maize and is ideal for corn bread, Mexican pancakes and various batters.

Buckwheat: Another meal used for pancakes, biscuits and various different breads.

Oats: These are coarser than flour and different grades are available to suit your baking requirements. Oats are very nutritious and are used in the making of flapjacks, porridge, muesli and many other recipes.

Bran: The fibre-rich outer casing of wheat used on its own as an addition to barn cakes, muffins, cereals, etc.

Wheatgerm: High in vitamins and natural oils, wheatgerm gives a nutty flavour to cereals and breads.

Malt flour: The dried powder produced from malted barley and wheat grains is high in diastatic sugars which develop the yeast to give better crusts. It imparts a malty sweet flavour to breads and confectionery.

Soya flour: Made from the soya bean, soya flour is rich in protein but low in gluten. It is extremely versatile and suitable for people on special diets. Use it in bread (1 tablespoon per 450g/1lb of flour) to improve the overall texture and flavour.

Raising Agents

Yeast: This is the core of, and essential raising agent in, breadmaking.

Yeast is a living cell and converts sugars in a dough to carbon dioxide and alcohol, the latter evaporating on baking. When flour, water, salt and yeast are joined together by mixing and kneading, the gas expands, stretching the glutenous strands which develop a cellular structure. The resultant dough is then *proved* (left in a warm place) and continues to rise. During baking the yeast expands the dough to its maximum and is then killed as the temperature rises. For bread with real flavour, prove for at least 1 hour or alternatively use an ascorbic acid tablet (vitamin C) as this will eliminate bulk fermentation and shorten the breadmaking time.

Yeast comes in three varieties — fresh compressed; dried granules; and instant powdered with vitamin C. Fresh is by far the best, being active instantly but with only a short shelf-life. It will, however, freeze. Dried yeast granules, dissolved in water, need time to activate but will keep for months in a dry place. A new powdered yeast with vitamin C not only cuts out the fermentation but also mixes in dry, without added water, straight from the packet. This can be used when the other forms are not available.

Baking powder: Unlike yeast, baking powder is a chemical. Like yeast, it aerates scones, cakes, sponges and pastry by producing carbon dioxide which expands the dough structure, resulting in light delicate morsels.

Sweetening Agents

Sugars: Unrefined, white caster or granulated are the most commonly used sweeteners in baking, although excessive use is discouraged on health grounds.

Raw sugar: This is unrefined and still contains some of the natural minerals. Use in fruit cakes, malt breads and dark toffees, etc.

Dark brown sugar: This contains a certain amount of moisture as well as minerals. Ideal for dark, rich fruit cakes, Christmas puddings, fudges and candies.

Demerara sugar: More refined than dark brown sugar, Demerara has brown crystals used mainly in coffee and as a decoration on cakes.

Note: Any of the sugars can be used in the recipes according to their role as either a sweetener or a decoration.

Muscovado sugar: This covers a range of partially refined or totally unrefined sugars used in wholefood preparations.

Mollasses: A dark brown tar-like syrup, used mainly in ginger cakes and biscuits and foods with a spicy content.

Treacle: A strong bitter-sweet dark syrup used to colour and sweeten.

Golden syrup: A refined syrup with a delicate flavour, used in puddings, tarts, spiced cakes and sweets.

Honey: Although a sweet product, honey is produced naturally by bees. It has a definite flavour and is famed for its use in many local specialities, e.g. Honey Cake, and is used in sponges, breads and desserts.

Fats and Shortening

Fats used in baking produce the necessary qualities to impart richness, shortness, volume and colour and to improve the shelf-life. The flavour required will determine whether butter or vegetable fat is used.

Butter: A dairy product which was the only fat used in baking until margarine came along. The flavour of butter carries right through to the finished baked article. Ideal for buttercream, puff and Danish pastry and cakes of all descriptions.

Lard: This is refined animal fat and used for its flavour in bread, lardy cakes, savoury pastry and general cooking. If you are concerned about the use of animal fats, substitute low polyunsaturated fats. The results will be just as good. Choose from vegetable margarine, olive, corn, nut and sunflower oils.

Other Major Ingredients

Salt: Bread without salt would be unbearable. Salt imparts and brings out the wholesome flavours of foods.

Skimmed milk powder: This is used to increase the food value and improves the crumb texture and crust appearance. Milk bread was very popular after World War II as the mineral content benefited children and the elderly.

Buttermilk: The milk from buttermaking makes delicious scones and soda bread. The lactic acid works with the bicarbonate of soda producing light, crumbly, traditional breads.

Fresh dairy cream: Single, double and whipping cream are all used in baking to fill and decorate many variations of cakes, sponges, gateaux and desserts. It also enriches and thickens sauces.

Eggs (yolks and whites):   These are used in all sorts of baked products. They enrich, aerate, stabilise and colour breads, cakes, sponges, meringues, sweets, desserts and sauces. Egg washes feature throughout the recipes. These are simply brushed on the tops of produce before baking to give a sheen. The eggs can be mixed with milk in order to go further.

Fruits: Fruits have been used extensively since our early trading days — choose from currants, sultanas, raisins, dates, apricots, prunes, cherries and angelica — and added to the more traditional native fruits, extend the range of baked goods open to you to make. High in vitamins and natural carbohydrates, fruit is an ideal addition to any confection.

Fresh fruits: In season fresh fruits are more appealing than dried in flans, pies, tarts and desserts.

Nuts: Full of protein, high in vitamin B and minerals, products containing nuts are very nutritious. Select from almonds, hazelnuts, walnuts, peanuts, cashews, brazils and coconuts.

Herbs: Fresh herbs are recommended throughout but a pinch of the dried equivalents will suffice in most cases if fresh herbs are unavailable.

Seeds: These have become more popular as an ingredient in baking in recent years. Starting with the white, nutty-flavoured sesame seeds, others include poppy, carraway, pumpkin, sunflower and many more. Use them to decorate and flavour breads, cakes and pastries.

Flavours: These can be added to improve the overall taste of what you bake. Not only can you use natural essences such as vanilla, lemon, orange, and almond but also, for a more exotic effect, add liqueurs to your cream creations.

Spices: These range from the basic mixed spice which is available ready-prepared in shops to the subtle flavours of cinnamon, mace, nutmeg, ginger, coriander and so on. Take care when measuring since too much spice tends to be bitter and impairs the finished product.

EQUIPMENT

A range of reliable equipment (including a good pair of hands!) will speed you along the dusty, floury road to success. The basic requirements are listed below.

Basic Equipment

Electric mixer: Make sure it will stand up to the stiff doughs you are making.

Mixing bowls: Very useful for all the mixing and for storage.

Set of scales: Check that they are accurate.

Rolling pin: Wooden, china or plastic will do. Make sure it is clean before use.

Whisk: A balloon shape is best for whisking meringues and creams.

Spatulas: Very useful tool — have several wooden or plastic ones handy.

Pastry brush: Used for glazing the tops of pastry. Bristle or nylon can be used.

Sharp knife: Essential! You will also need pastry cutters (round and other shapes); piping (or Savoy) bag; piping tubes (star and plain—metal or plastic); 1 litre or 2 pint measuring jug; baking sheets and trays; non-stick tins (although well oiled ordinary ones will do); a good sieve; double or single saucepans (copper for sugar boiling); sugar thermometer; oiled polythene sheets for covering dough; greaseproof paper.

Ovens

An important thing is a good oven — gas or electric will produce good results. Microwave ovens are now more familiar in many kitchens. Although they reduce baking times by many minutes, the results are often baked produce with very little crust colour and I would strongly suggest you finish the baking in a conventional oven. The new models, however, incorporate a facility that browns as well as cooks.

No doubt computers will make their appearance in the kitchen, too, soon. When I began baking in the fifties the only tools I could blame were a rolling pin, a sieve, a jug and a table and my chief resource was an awful lot of elbow grease!

However, the most valuable *ingredient* of all has always been *TIME!*

IMPORTANT NOTE

Both Metric and Imperial measurements have been included in all the recipes in this book. It is important when attempting a recipe to adhere to one set of measurements or the other and not to mix them, as they are not exact equivalents.

NOTE ON THE MICROWAVE OVEN

Many of the recipes in this book include details for using the microwave oven. It is important to note that the recipes were developed and tested using a 600 watt microwave oven, and that cooking times may need some adjustment depending on the model and wattage of the microwave being used.

Freezing

The recipes in this book are best eaten fresh on the day of making. Freezing times have been included, but are only approximate.

CHAPTER 1

ALL MANNA OF BREADS!

The mysteries of breadmaking go back a long way. Old fashioned crafts-men, although highly skilled bakers, lacked the technical knowledge which today has brought science into the kitchen. It wasn't long ago that bread was made without yeast. A 'barm', as it was called, was used to aerate the dough and was the forerunner to today's yeast. In those days the local brewer was very friendly with the baker, who would enjoy his popular brew in the bakehouse. The odd drop of ale would find its way into the dough and — unknown to the baker — fermentation began. An extract from *The London Art of Cookery* by John Farley in 1789 illustrates the method of making leaven bread at that time:

Bread made without barm must be by the assistance of leaven. Take a lump of dough, about two pounds of your last making, which has been raised by barm. Keep it by you in a wooden vessel, cover it well with flour, and this will be your leaven. The night before you intend to bake, put your leaven to a peck of flour, and work them well together with warm water. Let it lie in a dry wooden vessel, well covered with a linen cloth and a blanket, and keep it in a warm place. This dough, kept warm, will rise again next morning, and will be sufficient to mix with two or three bushels of flour, being mixed up with warm water and a little salt. When it be well worked up and thoroughly mix with the flour, let it be well covered with the linen and blanket, until you find it begin to rise. Then knead it well, and work it up into Bricks or Loaves, making the loaves Broad, and not so thick and high as is frequently done, by which means the bread will be better Baked. Always keep by you two or more pounds of the Dough of your Last baking well covered with flour, to make leaven to serve from one baking day to another; and the more leaven you put to the flour, the Lighter the bread will be. The fresher the leaven, the less sour will be the bread.

In this chapter you can try the simpler recipes or the more adventurous ones. All they need is time, warmth and a little skill. And remember, if you fail once, try again. Your endeavour will be rewarded.

Country Manor Bread

Makes 2 loaves   Preparation time: 2 hours   Baking time: 30 minutes

A white speckled loaf for those who like white bread with the added goodness of wheatgerm and rye flakes.

For the bread:
1kg/2lb 4oz untreated white strong
  flour
2 teaspoons salt
25g/1oz milk powder
25g/1oz lard or white shortening
25g/1oz wheatgerm
25g/1oz rye flakes
40g/1½oz yeast
625ml/1 pint 2fl oz warm water

For the topping:
3 tablespoons milk
50g/2oz wheat flakes

Use a 30cm/12in baking sheet, well oiled

Pre-heat the oven to 230°C/450°F/Gas Mark 8
Microwave: Bake bread for 4 minutes on low setting and then transfer to conventional oven for 15 minutes at above temperature to achieve a brown, crusty finish.

1   Mix together the flour, salt and milk powder in a mixing bowl. Add the lard, wheatgerm and rye flakes. Combine well.

2   Disperse the yeast in the water and add to the dry ingredients. Mix into a smooth, elastic dough for 10 minutes. Leave in the bowl and cover with a damp cloth. Prove for 1 hour in a warm place.

3   After 1 hour divide the dough into 2 × 1kg/2lb pieces and mould into round shapes. Place onto the greased baking sheet and score down the middle with a sharp knife. Then cut on the slant either side of the centre line to give a leaf-like design to the top.

4   Prove for 40 minutes further. Then glaze the top with milk and sprinkle wheat flakes on. Bake in the oven for 30 minutes or microwave as above.

Secret tip: Make sure the water is warm (27 °C/85 °F) as the yeast will not work in cold water.

Serving suggestion: Cut slices of the bread and lightly butter them. Place two strips of anchovy on the bread with a slice of tomato and a spoonful of coleslaw. Eat as an open sandwich with a glass of real ale.

Freezing: If you cut the loaf before freezing it will mean you can avoid defrosting the whole loaf. In this way you can just take what you want. Country Manor Bread will keep for up to 3 months in the freezer.

Farm-Mill Morning Rolls

Makes 32 rolls   Preparation time: 2½ hours   Baking time: 20 minutes

A tempting way to start the day. A soft, light textured roll which cries out for attention. Just cut and layer with farm butter and homemade marmalade. Scrumptious!

For the rolls:
1.1kg/2lb 6oz untreated strong
  white flour
2 teaspoons salt
40g/1½oz milk powder
40g/1½oz lard or white
  shortening
40g/1½oz yeast
700ml/1 pint 4fl oz warm water
1 teaspoon malt extract
1 ascorbic acid tablet (vitamin C)

For the topping:
75g/3oz sieved flour

Use a 30cm/12in baking sheet, well oiled

Pre-heat the oven to 230°C/450°F/Gas Mark 8
Microwave: Bake rolls for 2 minutes on low setting and then transfer to the conventional oven for 10 minutes at above temperature to achieve a brown crusty finish.

---

1   Blend together together the flour, salt and milk powder in a mixing bowl. Add the lard.

---

2   Disperse the yeast in the warm water together with the malt extract and the vitamin C tablet. Add to the dry ingredients. Knead by hand to a smooth elastic dough for 10 minutes, or 3 minutes in a food processor. Leave in the bowl and cover with a damp cloth. Rest for 10 minutes in a warm place.

---

3   Proceed to scale the dough into 32 equal pieces. Mould these into round balls. Place on the oiled baking sheet smooth side up. Cover with an oiled polythene sheet to prevent skinning.

---

4   Prove the dough balls in a warm place for 40 minutes and then dust the tops with the sieved flour. Microwave as above or bake normally for 15—20 minutes. The farm-mill rolls should be lightly baked with a soft crust.

Secret tip: A bowl of hot water placed in the oven 10 minutes prior to baking will ensure a soft roll. It also acts as a prover. Make sure the bowl is removed 5 minutes after placing the rolls in the oven for the final baking.

Serving suggestion: Cut the rolls in half and butter them. Place 2 slices of grilled bacon, a chopped, fried mushroom and a cut boiled egg on top. Add a little mayonnaise and there you have a Bac-room Meggy!

Freezing: When cold, place the farm-mill rolls in polythene bags and keep in the freezer for up to 2 months. To freshen just microwave for 40 seconds.

Malted Saxon Loaf

Makes 4 × 1lb loaves   Preparation time: 2½ hours   Baking time: 30 minutes

This has been adapted from an old English recipe brought up to date for those who like malted whole grains with a hint of honey.

For the pre-mix:
*75g/3oz wholewheat grains (or
 barley)*
1 tablespoon liquid malt extract
25g/1oz honey
50g/2oz warm water

For the dough:
*800g/1lb 12oz wheatmeal strong
 flour*
100g/4oz rye flour
2 teaspoons salt
25g/1oz milk powder
25g/1oz lard or white shortening
25g/1oz yeast
575ml/1 pint warm water
The pre-mix

For the topping:
3 tablespoons milk/egg
75g/3oz cracked wholewheat

Use a 30cm/12in baking sheet, well oiled

Pre-heat the oven to 220°C/425°F/Gas Mark 7
Microwave: Bake loaf for 3 minutes on low setting and then transfer to the conventional oven for 15 minutes at above temperature to produce a rustic brown crust.

---

1   For the pre-mix, soak the wholewheat grains, malt extract and honey in the warm water for 2—4 hours.

---

2   Mix together the wheatmeal, rye flour, salt and add the milk powder in a mixing bowl. Add the lard and blend in.

---

3   Disperse the pre-mix throughout the dry ingredients.

---

4 Dissolve the yeast in the water and add to the dry ingredients. Mix by hand to a smooth elastic dough for 10 minutes, or 3—5 minutes in a food processor. Leave in the bowl and cover with a damp cloth. Prove for 1 hour in a warm place.

5 Scale the dough into 4 pieces and mould them into rounds. Rest for 5 minutes and then roll out flat to a thickness of 2.5cm/1 in. Place onto the baking sheet smooth-side up. Use a knife to divide the loaf into 4 equal sections. Cover with an oiled polythene sheet to prevent skinning.

6 Glaze the top with the milk/egg and sprinkle cracked wholewheat all over. Prove in a warm place for about 40 minutes. Microwave as above or bake normally for 30—40 minutes.

Secret tip: If you prefer, a vitamin C tablet added to the water will cut out the proving time.

Serving suggestion: Malted Saxon Loaf marries well with smoked cheese and the piquancy of freshly made tomato chutney.

Freezing: The loaf will keep in the freezer for up to 3 months.

Castle Grain Bread

Makes 4 × 450g/1lb loaves   Preparation time: 2½ hours
Baking time: 30 minutes

In the days of yore the miller was known to adulterate the flour by using bean-meal, chalk or even ashes of bones. Today only certain additives are permitted, chalk being one. In this recipe we use only untreated flour with a little dash of natural grain.

For the bread:
900g/2lb untreated strong white
 flour
100g/4oz mixed grain, crushed
 (wheat, barley, rye, oats or
 buckwheat)
2 teaspoons salt
25g/1oz lard or white shortening
40g/1½oz yeast
1 teaspoon honey
625ml/1 pint 2fl oz warm water
1 tablespoon carraway seeds

For the topping:
3 tablespoons milk/egg
75g/3oz rolled oats

Use 2 × 30cm/12in baking sheets, well oiled

Pre-heat the oven to 220°C/425°F/Gas Mark 7
Microwave: Bake loaf for 5 minutes on low setting and then transfer to the conventional oven for 15 minutes at above temperature to create a light, golden loaf.

---

1 Mix together the flour, mixed grains and salt in a mixing bowl. Add the lard and blend in.

---

2 Dissolve the yeast and honey in the water and add to the dry ingredients. Mix and knead by hand for 10 minutes, or for 3—5 minutes in the food processor, until the dough is developed. Finally add the carraway seeds and mix to disperse. Leave in the bowl and cover with a damp cloth. Prove for 1 hour in a warm place.

3   Scale the dough into 4 pieces. Mould these into round shapes and then rest for 5 minutes. Then roll each piece out into a long stick. From the end of each stick cut a small piece of dough (25g/1oz) and mould these smaller pieces into rounds. The remaining sticks are then made into a circle or ring and joined together. Place the 4 small rolls at equal intervals around the ring like 4 turrets on a castle wall. With your finger push into the centre of each 'turret' to seal it to the 'wall'. Transfer to a well greased baking sheet. Use a pair of scissors to snip smaller turrets into the walls between your 4 main ones. Cover with an oiled polythene sheet to prevent skinning.

4   Glaze the top with the milk/egg and sprinkle rolled oats over the 4 turrets. Prove in a warm place for about 40 minutes. Microwave as above, or bake as normal for 35—40 minutes.

Secret tip: Instead of mixed grains use chopped mixed nuts or various seeds to impart a wholesome nutty flavour. Remember, if you use dried yeast, use only half the amount compared to fresh baker's yeast which is already active for baking.

Serving suggestion: Castle Grain Bread is ideal for parties as a showpiece. In the central ring place a yoghurt dip, and in another bowl some mixed cut carrots, celery and so on. The bread can then be broken up and used in the dip.

Freezing: Will keep in the freezer for up to 2 months.

Wholemeal Baps and Batons

Makes 30 Baps or 16 Batons   Preparation time: 2½ hours
Baking time: 20 minutes

Children love soft baps. Made with 100% wholemeal flour, these not only taste good but contain natural fibre for health. Let's get bapping!

For the baps/batons:
900g/2lb 100% wholemeal flour
2 teaspoons salt
40g/1½oz milk powder
25g/1oz sugar
40g/1½oz white shortening
40g/1½oz yeast
625ml/1 pint 2fl oz warm water
1 tablespoon sesame seeds

For the topping:
3 tablespoons milk/egg
75g/3oz sesame seeds

Use 2 x 30cm/12in baking sheets, well oiled

Pre-heat the oven to 230°C/450°F/Gas Mark 8
Microwave: Bake the baps/batons for 2 minutes on low setting then transfer to the conventional oven for 10 minutes at the above temperature.

---

1   Combine the flour, salt, milk powder and sugar in a mixing bowl. Add the shortening and blend in.

---

2   Dissolve the yeast in the water and add to the dry ingredients. Mix and knead by hand for 10 minutes, or 3—5 minutes in the food processor, until the dough is developed. Finally add the sesame seeds and mix to disperse. Leave in the bowl and cover with a damp cloth. Prove for 1 hour in a warm place.

---

3   Scale the dough into 30 pieces, or mould into 16 round shapes if you are making the batons. Rest for 5 minutes then roll out into flat pancakes for baps. For the batons roll to the shape of a cigar.

4   'Egg wash' (i.e. using the milk/egg mix), the tops and dip into sesame seeds. Transfer to well greased baking sheets. Cover with an oiled polythene sheet to prevent skinning. Prove in a warm place for about 35 minutes. Microwave as above, or bake normally for 15—20 minutes.

Secret tip: The microwave oven will produce a satisfactory result using 100% wholemeal flour, but white flour bread and rolls tend to lack crust colour.

Serving suggestion: Marinade slices of smoked salmon in dry white wine and a little crushed garlic and dill for a couple of hours. Layer baps or batons with the salmon and top with a little cream cheese; leave open or make lids with the other half of the rolls to produce a burger with a difference!

Freezing: Will keep in the freezer for up to 2 months. Always store in polythene bags to prevent drying out.

Traditional Rural Cottage Loaf

Makes 2 × 1kg/2lb loaves   Preparation time: 2 hours   Baking time: 35 minutes

An example of a true English country loaf, not easy to make but well worth a try if you follow my simple guide. Like all bread, time and warmth is required, with a little energy, to produce wonderful results.

For the bread:
*1kg/2lb 4oz untreated strong
   white flour*
2 teaspoons salt
25g/1oz milk powder
25g/1oz white shortening
40g/1½oz yeast
625ml/1 pint 2fl oz warm water

For the topping:
3 tablespoons milk/egg
50g/2oz poppy seeds

Use 2 × 30cm/12in baking sheets, well oiled

Pre-heat the oven to 230°C/450°F/Gas Mark 8
Microwave: Bake cottage loaf for 3 minutes on low setting and then transfer to the conventional oven for 15 minutes at above temperature till baked.

---

1   Combine the flour, salt and milk powder in a mixing bowl. Add the shortening and blend in.

---

2   Dissolve the yeast in the water and add to the dry ingredients. Mix and knead by hand for 10 minutes, or for 3—5 minutes in the food processor, until the dough is developed. Dough temperature should be slightly warm (27°C/80°F). Leave in the bowl and cover with a damp cloth. Prove for 1 hour like this in a warm place.

---

3   Divide the dough into 2 equal pieces. Cut each piece of the dough so that the 'top' of the eventual loaf weighs about 275g/10oz and the 'bottom' about 600g/1lb 6oz. Mould into round shapes and rest for 5 minutes. Egg wash the tops and place the smaller piece on top of the larger one. Slightly flatten both top and bottom. With the tip of the finger press into the centre right through the centre to the bottom to seal the sections together.

---

4 Egg wash the tops again and dip into poppy seeds. Transfer to well greased baking sheets. Cover with an oiled polythene sheet to prevent skinning.

5 Prove in a warm place for about 45 minutes. If the top appears to be toppling over gently reposition by pressing the finger in the centre. Rest for a few minutes. Microwave as above or bake normally for 30—35 minutes.

Secret tip: If the cottage loaf is not fully proved the top will tend to separate when baking. Make sure the dough is not too soft. It should be fairly tight. Try making cottage rolls — the principle is the same.

Serving suggestion: Simply lashings of farm butter and Granny's special strawberry and quince jam.

Freezing: Will keep in the freezer for up to 3 months, but I suggest you eat the same day as baking.

Viking Long Boats

Makes 6 × 450g/1lb loaves   Preparation time: 2½ hours
Baking time: 35 minutes

If you like rye bread, this is for you. Back in feudal times when flavour was the order of the day, Vikings returned home after a hard day at battle demanding their favourite rye bread. See if you can conquer this recipe.

Pre-mix sour dough:
15g/½oz yeast
350ml/12fl oz water
350g/12oz rye flour

For the bread:
900g/2lb untreated strong white
  flour
350g/12oz rye flour
3 teaspoons salt
25g/1oz white shortening
625ml/1 pint 2fl oz warm water
1 tablespoon carraway seeds

For the topping:
3 tablespoons milk/egg
75g/3oz poppy seeds

Use 2 × 30cm/12in baking sheets, well oiled

Pre-heat the oven to 220°C/425°F/Gas Mark 7
Microwave: Bake for 3 minutes on low setting and then transfer to the conventional oven for 15 minutes at the above temperature until baked. For best results I recommend baking in a convector oven.

---

1 Pre-mix sour dough. Dissolve the yeast in the water and add to the rye flour. Mix together to form a dough. Leave to mature overnight.

---

2 Blend together the flour, rye flour and salt in mixing bowl. Add the shortening and blend in.

---

3   Pour the water into the above mixture. Add the sour dough and mix/knead for 10 minutes, or 3—5 minutes in a food processor until the dough is developed. Add the carraway seeds and blend them in. The dough temperature should be 27°C/80°F. Leave in the bowl covered with a damp cloth to prove for 1 hour in a warm place.

4   Divide the dough into 6 pieces. Mould each into a round and rest for 5 minutes. Roll out the dough to the shape of a boat (baton) and make 5 cuts slantwise across the top.

5   Egg wash the tops and dip into poppy seeds or carraway seeds. Transfer to the greased baking sheets. Cover with an oiled polythene sheet to prevent skinning. Prove in a warm place for 30—35 minutes.

Secret tip: Use the microwave to speed up the proving time. Place dough in an oiled polythene bag and microwave for 30 seconds — then 30 seconds in the 'off' position, and repeat this operation until the dough has doubled in volume. Make sure the dough is not too soft — it should be fairly tight.

Serving suggestion: With a sharp knife, cut out the centre of each roll like the hull of a boat. Make various sandwiches with the cut out pieces and return to the boat. Place a long cheese straw in the centre and wait for the invasion!

Freezing: Will keep in the freezer for up to 3 months.

Aberdeen Hearth Bread

Makes 3 loaves   Preparation time: 2 hours   Baking time: 30 minutes

Rob Roy favoured this type of loaf whilst in exile. It has a subtle taste with a good shelf-life. All bonnie lads and lasses enjoy it!

For the bread:
850g/1lb 14oz 100% wholemeal
  flour
550g/1lb 4oz strong white flour
25g/1oz milk powder
3 teaspoons salt
25g/1oz white shortening
50g/2oz yeast
850ml/1 pint 10 fl oz warm
  water
1 egg
1 tablespoon treacle
1 tablespoon cracked wheat

For the topping:
3 tablespoons milk/egg
75g/3oz cracked wheat

Use 2 × 30cm/12in baking sheets, well oiled

Pre-heat the oven to 230°C/450°F/Gas Mark 8
Microwave: Bake for 3 minutes on low setting and then transfer to a conventional oven for 15 minutes at the above temperature until baked.

---

1   Mix the wholemeal flour, white flour, milk powder and salt together. Blend in the shortening.

---

2   Soak the yeast in the water and add the egg and treacle. Pour onto dry ingredients and mix together to form a smooth dough. Add the cracked wheat and rest for 15 minutes.

---

3   Divide the dough into 3 pieces. Mould into round shapes and rest for 5 minutes. Roll out the dough to the shape of a baton and make a cut down the centre of each.

4   Egg wash the tops and dip into cracked wheat. Transfer to the baking sheets
    and cover with an oiled polythene sheet to prevent skinning. Prove in a warm
    place for 35 minutes. Microwave as above or bake normally for 30—35
    minutes.

Secret tip: If you do not intend to bake on the same day, place the dough in
an oiled polythene bag and leave overnight in the fridge. Bring to room temperature
before shaping.

Serving suggestion: Cut the Aberdeen Hearth Loaf down the middle and lightly spread a mixture of soft butter and horseradish sauce on each side. Layer with
slices of Scotch beef and you'll hear the distant drums of the clans approaching!

Freezing: Will keep in the freezer for up to 3 months.

Oasthouse Ale Bread

Makes 2 loaves   Preparation time: 2 hours   Baking time: 30 minutes

On a visit to Kent and their many real alehouses, one can't resist the urge to sample the local brew, together with a fresh crusty morsel of wholemeal bread. What a good idea for a recipe...

For the bread:
900g/2lb 100% wholemeal flour
2 teaspoons salt
25g/1oz lard or white shortening
25g/1oz yeast
275ml/10fl oz warm water
1 tablespoon malt extract
1 tablespoon honey
275ml/10fl oz real ale

For the topping:
3 tablespoons real ale
1 tablespoon honey
75g/3oz toasted rolled oats

Use 2 × 900g/2lb loaf tins, well oiled and warm

Pre-heat the oven to 230°C/450°F/Gas Mark 8
Microwave: Not recommended unless special microwave containers are used.

---

1   Mix the wholemeal flour and salt together. Blend in the lard or white shortening.

2   Soak the yeast in the water and add the malt extract and honey. Pour onto the dry ingredients. Add the real ale and mix together to form a smooth, elastic dough. Prove the dough in an oiled polythene bag for 30 minutes or until it has risen.

3   Knockback (beat the dough) to expel all the air and rest the dough for 10 minutes. Divide the dough into 2 pieces and mould into round shapes. Rest for 5 minutes. Flatten and roll out the dough Swiss-roll fashion to the shape of a sausage. Place in warm loaf tins smooth-side up. Cover with oiled polythene sheet.

4   Prove in a warm place for 35 minutes or till well risen. Bake normally for
    30-35 minutes as above.

5   When the loaves are baked and still hot, brush with the real ale and honey
    mixed together over the tops. Sprinkle with roasted rolled oats and leave to cool.

Secret tip: If you have any flat ale over from a party then use in this recipe,
as it develops a stronger flavour than otherwise. Makes tasty rolls too.

Serving suggestion: Go rural — a chunk of well-matured Stilton, a home-pickled
onion and a yard of Oasthouse ale.

Freezing: Will keep in the freezer for up to 3 months.

Ploughman's Revenge

Makes 8   Preparation time: 2½ hours   Baking time: 25 minutes

As a boy I remember working for long days harvesting the wheat. My particular recollection is of a giant package of delicate crust enclosing a mixture of farm vegetables and freshly curded cheese which was our lunch. It was always a welcome break. Harvesting will never be the same!

For the bread crust:
450g/1lb strong white flour
½ teaspoon of salt
2 teaspoons milk powder
50g/2fl oz vegetable oil
1 egg
25g/1oz yeast
225ml/8fl oz warm water

For the filling:
450g/1lb potatoes, part-boiled
  and cubed
100g/4oz carrots, cooked and
  cubed
100/4oz celery, cooked and
  cubed
50g/2oz haricot beans, soaked
  and cooked
50g/2oz swede, cooked and
  cubed
50g/2oz onion, cooked and sliced
  100g/4oz Lymeswold or similar
  soft cheese, chopped
Pinch of salt and pepper
½ teaspoon of mixed herbs

For the glaze:
1 tablespoon milk
1 beaten egg
Pinch of sugar

Use 2 × 30cm/12in baking sheets

Pre-heat the oven to 200°C/400°F/Gas Mark 6
Microwave: 3 minutes on low setting and then transfer to conventional oven for 10—15 minutes or until golden brown.

1 Mix the flour, salt and milk powder and then add the oil. Blend thoroughly.

2 Add the egg and yeast to the water and pour onto the above mixture, stirring well. Knead to a smooth, elastic dough. Place in an oiled polythene bag and prove until well risen.

3 Divide the dough into 8 pieces and mould into round balls. Rest for 5 minutes. Lightly dust with flour and roll out flat in circular shapes to a thickness of 5mm/¼ in. Egg wash the edges.

4 For the filling mix all the cooked ingredients together. Season with the salt, pepper and herbs.

5 Place a portion of filling on the 8 breadcrust circles and turn over as for pasties. Seal the edges by pinching to produce a crimped pattern. Pierce the top to allow the steam to escape. Egg wash and place on the baking sheets. Prove for 30 minutes before baking.

Secret tip: Instead of cheese, use corned beef or boiled ham with a hint of mustard as a seasoning.

Serving suggestion: A tossed salad of endive and tomatoes in a garlic vinaigrette. Serve on an oval platter. Happy harvest time!

Freezing: These bread rounds will keep unfilled for up to 3 months in the freezer.

Cider Clove Ring Bread

Makes 2 loaves   Preparation time: 2 hours   Baking time: 30 minutes

A traditional-type bread based around the very potent Devonshire scrumpy.

For the bread:
675g/1lb 8oz wheatmeal flour
1 teaspoon salt
1 tablespoon milk powder
25g/1oz vegetable oil
25g/1oz yeast
275ml/10fl oz warm water
1 tablespoon honey
100ml/4fl oz cider or scrumpy
50g/2oz dried apples
3—4 cloves
Pinch of nutmeg

For the topping:
3 tablespoons milk/egg
50g/2oz apples, chopped

For the glaze:
50ml/2fl oz cider
1 tablespoon honey

Use 2 × 450g/1lb round ring loaf tins, well oiled and warm

Pre-heat the oven to 220°C/425°F/Gas Mark 7
Microwave: Not recommended unless special microwave containers are used.

---

1 Mix the wheatmeal flour, salt and milk powder together. Blend in the oil.

2 Soak the yeast in the water and add the honey. Pour onto the dry ingredients. Add the cider and mix together to form a smooth, elastic dough (about 10 minutes by hand or 3—5 minutes in a food processor).

3 Soak the dried apples and cloves to soften. Strain. Add to the dough with a pinch of nutmeg. Combine well. Prove the dough in an oiled polythene bag for 30 minutes, till risen.

4 Knockback and rest for 10 minutes. Divide the dough into 2 pieces. Mould into round shapes and rest for 5 minutes. Flatten and roll out the dough Swiss-roll fashion to the shape of a sausage. Place in warm round ring loaf tins smooth-side up. Cut with a pair of clean scissors to make a pattern around the edge.

5 Scatter apples over the top and press into the surface. Bake normally, for 30—35 minutes.

6 When the loaves are baked and still hot, brush the surface with cider/honey mixture.

Secret tip: The knockback helps to develop the dough, resulting in a well baked loaf. Use chopped apricots as an alternative to apples.

Serving suggestion: Chop equal amounts of apples, celery and some croutons. Place in a bowl and mix in some cider vinaigrette, a pinch of paprika and spoon into the centre of the ring. A smash at parties!

Freezing: Will keep in the freezer for up to 3 months.

English Heritage Leaven Bread

Makes 3 loaves   Preparation time: 2½ hours   Baking time: 35 minutes

Many years ago the local village baker used a leaven to aerate his doughs. It is said that whilst slurping ale, a portion ended up in the flour! Unknown to him, the bread improved and as the ale flowed, yeast was born.

For the pre-overnight leaven:
450g/1lb strong white flour
½ teaspoon salt
Pinch of yeast
275ml/10fl oz cool water

25g/1oz lard
25g/1oz yeast
575ml/1 pint warm water

For the bread:
1kg/2lb 2 oz untreated strong
  white flour

For the glaze:
75ml/3fl oz boiled water
25g/1oz potato starch

Use 2 × 30cm/12in baking sheets, well oiled

Pre-heat the oven to 230°C/450°F/Gas Mark 8
Microwave: 3 minutes on low setting then transfer to the conventional oven for 10—15 minutes or until golden brown.

1   For the overnight leaven, mix the flour and the salt. Dissolve the yeast in the water and add the flour. Mix well to a smooth dough. Place in an oiled polythene bag and leave overnight in a warm place.

2   For the bread, mix the flour and fat. Disperse the yeast in the water and add to the dry ingredients. Add the overnight leaven and mix all well together to make a smooth elastic dough. Rest for 10 minutes.

3   Divide in to 3 pieces. Shape each into round cobs and rest for 5 minutes. Press out flat and roll up Swiss-roll fashion into a sausage about 25cm/10in long. Glaze the top and make 8 slanted cuts along the top. Place on a baking tray. Cover with oiled polythene and prove for 40 minutes. For best results glaze again with potato starch. Bake until a golden crust forms.

Secret tip: To check the loaf, tap the bottom. If it sounds hollow, it is baked.

Serving suggestion: A slice of this bread with a little butter is all you knead!

Freezing: Keeps for up to 3 months but not recommended.

Aunt Jacey's Malt Bread

Makes 4 loaves   Preparation time: 2 hours   Baking time: 35 minutes

Every Sunday it was always a treat when my Aunt Jacey passed the slices of toasted malt bread around. She had a knack of making it taste like nectar on the tongue. My sister wasn't keen — which meant all the more for me!

For the bread:
750g/1lb 11oz wholemeal flour
225g/8oz strong white flour
2 teaspoons salt
25g/1oz shortening
25g/1oz yeast
575ml/1 pint warm water

1 tablespoon honey
1 tablespoon treacle
50ml/1fl oz liquid malt extract
275g/10oz sultanas
50g/2oz chopped almonds

Use 4 × 450g/1lb loaf tins, well oiled

Pre-heat the oven to 200°C/400°F/Gas Mark 6
Microwave: 3 minutes on low setting then transfer to a conventional oven for 10—15 minutes. Use a dual purpose loaf tin as microwaves don't take to metal containers.

1   Mix the flours, salt and fat together. Dissolve the yeast in the water with the honey, treacle and malt. Add to the flour and mix well to a smooth dough. Disperse the sultanas and chopped almonds in the dough. Cover and prove for 30 minutes.

2   Divide into 4 pieces and shape to fit the warmed loaf tins. This dough is rather sticky so take care when handling.

3   Cover with oiled polythene and prove for 40 minutes. Bake in a moderate overn.

Secret tip: By increasing the malt content you can determine whether it will be a light, medium or heavy loaf. The heavier the loaf, the lower the baking temperature.

Serving suggestion: A slice with cottage cheese and a spoon of honey is all you need for a healthy snack. Improves on keeping.

Freezing: Up to 3 months.

Basic Savoury Cheese Bread

Makes 3 loaves   Preparation time: 2 hours   Baking time: 30 minutes

The distinctive flavour of this loaf will appeal to lovers of cheese. By adjusting the seasoning you can create many variations. Try a little herb or spices to heighten the pleasure.

For the bread:
550g/1lb 4oz strong white flour
25g/1oz milk powder
½ teaspoon salt
½ teaspoon sugar
25g/1oz white shortening
225g/8oz grated Cheddar cheese

25g/1oz yeast
350ml/12fl oz warm water

For the glaze:
1 tablespoon milk
1 egg

Use 3 × 450g/1lb loaf tins, well oiled

Pre-heat the oven to 220°C/425°F/Gas Mark 7
Microwave: 3 minutes on low setting than transfer to conventional oven for 10—15 minutes. Use a dual purpose loaf tin, as microwaves don't like metal ones.

---

1 Mix the flour, milk powder, salt, sugar and fat together. Blend in the cheese.

---

2 Dissolve the yeast in the water. Add to the flour and mix well to a smooth dough. Cover and prove for 45 minutes.

---

3 Divide into 3 pieces and shape to fit the warmed loaf tin. Egg wash the tops, with the milk and egg mixed.

---

4 Cover with oiled polythene and prove for 40 minutes. Bake as above.

Secret tip: Sprinkle some grated cheese over the top towards the end of baking and serve hot with eggs Florentine.

Serving suggestion: Cut slices into small cubes and then deep fry for a few minutes in oil. These croutons can be used in soups, salads, sauces and dips. Children love them instead of crisps.

Freezing: Up to 3 months.

Garlic Carraway Seed Bread

Makes 4 loaves   Preparation time: 1 hour   Baking time: 30 minutes

If you are fond of garlic then this recipe is for you. Use the Basic Cheese Bread on page 38.

For the bread:
*1.5kg/3lb Basic Cheese Bread
  (page 38)*

½ teaspoon carraway seeds

For the filling:
*100g/4oz butter
2 cloves garlic, crushed
1 tablespoon fresh parsley,
  chopped*

For the glaze:
*1 tablespoon milk
1 egg*

Use 2 × 30cm/12in baking sheets, well oiled

Pre-heat the oven to 220°C/425°F/Gas Mark 7
Microwave: 3 minutes on low setting then transfer to conventional oven for 10—15 minutes.

1   Beat the butter, add the garlic, parsley and carraway seeds. Disperse well.

2   Divide the dough into 4 pieces and mould into a round. Rest for 5 minutes Roll out flat and egg wash with the glaze.

3   Spoon a portion of butter into the centre and enclose. Seal and roll out to the shape of a baton. Make 3 cuts on the top. Egg wash. Cover with oiled polythene and prove for 40 minutes. Bake as above.

Secret tip: Instead of filling before baking, cut open a baked baton and spread the butter inside. Wrap in tin foil and bake in a hot oven for 10 minutes. Serve immediately. Substitute sesame seeds for carraway seeds to give a more neutral flavour.

Serving suggestion: A plate of lasagne and oodles of garlic bread, a glass of wine and a little love and affection complete an evening!

Freezing: Up to 3 months.

Tudor Crescents

Makes 8 crescents   Preparation time: 1 hour   Baking time: 20 minutes

A combination of spinach and Stilton make these crescents ideally suited for those who seek inner strength.

For the crescents:
450g/1lb Basic Savoury Cheese
dough (page 38)

1 boiled egg, chopped
25g/1oz chives, chopped
Pinch of salt and pepper to taste

The filling:
100g/4oz spinach, cooked and
chopped
50g/2oz Stilton cheese, grated
50g/2oz soured cream or yoghurt

For the glaze:
1 tablespoon milk
1 egg
50g/2oz sesame seeds

Use a 30cm/12in baking sheet, well oiled

Pre-heat the oven to 200°C/400°F/Gas Mark 6
Microwave: 3 minutes on low setting then transfer to the conventional oven for 10—15 minutes.

1   Mix the spinach, Stilton and cream or yoghurt together. Add the chopped egg and chives. Season and disperse well.

2   Roll out the dough to a round flat shape (approximately 5mm/¼in thick). Divide into 8 portions and cut each into triangular shapes. Egg wash edges.

3   Spoon a portion of filling into the centre and roll up from the widest part, enclosing the spinach with the point at the top. Transfer to baking sheet.

4   Glaze the tops with egg and sprinkle sesame seeds over the top of each one. Prove for 30 minutes in a warm place. Bake till golden brown.

Secret tip: Add chopped cashew nuts for a crunchy difference. As an alternative, divide the dough into 2, line a 20cm/8in pie dish and fill the pie with spinach filling. Cover with the remaining dough. Egg wash, prove and bake.

Serving suggestion: Serve hot or cold as a light bite or as a starter to the main meal with a light ginger yoghurt sauce.

Freezing: Up to 3 months.

Meadow Platter

Makes 2   Preparation time: 1 hour   Baking time: 30 minutes

The mist lies close to the muddy ground and a new morning brings fresh and tender mushrooms. They are used to great effect in this recipe.

For the platter:
450g/1lb Basic Savoury Cheese
  dough (page 38)

For the filling:
225g/8oz dark mushrooms,
  cooked and chopped
50g/2oz bacon, lightly fried and
  chopped
½ onion

25g/1oz butter
Pinch of salt and pepper
150g/5oz double cream or
  yoghurt
1 tablespoon wine or Madeira

For the decoration:
1 tablespoon milk
1 egg
Sprig of watercress
2 radishes

Use 2 × 20cm/8in pie plates, well oiled

Pre-heat the oven to 200°C/400°F/Gas Mark 6
Microwave: 6 minutes on high setting, to bake completely, or 30 minutes in the conventional oven.

---

1   Sauté the mushrooms for a few seconds and then transfer to a bowl. Lightly fry the bacon and the onion in the butter. Add the mushrooms. Season. Pour the cream or yoghurt and the wine or Madeira over the mixture. Cook for 1 minute.

---

2   Roll out the dough to a round flat shape (5mm/¼in thick). Line the pie platters with it and pour the cooked mixture evenly over. Egg wash the edges.

---

3   Decorate with radish slices cut into star-shapes in a decorative pattern. Rest for 30 minutes and then bake at a moderate heat (see above). Finish with a sprig of watercress in the centre.

Secret tip: Instead of radish, use slices of tomato or boiled egg. Alternatively cover with the remainder of the dough. Egg wash, prove and bake. This will make 1 platter.

Serving suggestion: Serve hot or cold. This is ideal for picnics and parties.

Freezing: Up to 2 months.

CHAPTER 2

SWEET TEA BREADS AND BUNS

The nutritional value of bread can be increased by the addition of butter, milk, sugar, malt, fruit, nuts and seeds. In this chapter all the breads are enriched to make them a complete, energy-giving food. These additions help them to produce a softer crumb, a shorter crust, a sweeter taste and they also improve the keeping qualities of things like tea breads.

In England, the traditonal bun evolved from pancakes or fritters which were cooked on bakestones. Having no cover over them, the buns needed to be turned to complete cooking. It was not until the turn of the seventeenth century that ovens were used to produce the now popular bun. In Scotland the Black Bun, composed entirely of dried fruits and spices, differs greatly from the bun breads of Yorkshire, Lancashire and Ireland, where a softer and lighter bun is preferred.

The Hot Cross Bun originated as a round type of bread, having pagan rather than Christian associations. In early times it represented the sun and was offered as part of a ritual as a thanksgiving token. The cross divided the bun into four sections, each representing one of the four seasons. Even before Christ, the Romans marked the bread with a cross to ward off evil spirits that might enter the oven and affect the texture of the baked bread. These customs continued throughout the Middle Ages. Today you can see the cross on a Coburg loaf.

Superstitions surrounding bread continued to play a big part in the lives of the people in the role of offering a cure for many diseases. The bread itself was mixed with various 'healing' brews and then administered to the suffering.

The tradition to bake on Good Friday was hailed as a protection against evil. One bun was kept aside until the following year and it is thought that this annual preoccupation has continued to the present day in some parts. The crucifixion of Christ is generally believed to be the reason why we put the cross on buns. Like the poppy on Remembrance Day, the cross signifies Hope and Salvation, and offers a chance to reflect our intentions over the year ahead. An accepted tradition today, we munch our way through dozens of spicy Hot Cross Buns every year, but be sure to keep one back to ward off evil spirits!

Special Dinner Rolls

Makes 20   Preparation time: 2 hours   Baking time: 15—20 minutes

The first impression at a dinner party should always be the taste and freshness of the rolls, for they are often eaten whilst waiting for the main feast.

For the rolls:
500g/1lb 2oz strong white flour
1 teaspoon salt
15g/½oz sugar
15g/½oz shortening
25g/1oz yeast
275ml/½ pint warm water or
*   milk*

For the topping:
1 egg
50g/2oz sesame seeds or poppy
*   seeds*

Use 2 × 30cm/12in baking sheets, well oiled

Pre-heat the oven to 230°C/450°F/Gas Mark 8
Microwave: Approximately 6 minutes baked on special microwave ware.

1   Blend together the flour, salt, sugar and add the fat. Soak the yeast in the water or milk and add to the mixture. Knead for 10 minutes by hand or 3 minutes in the food processor until smooth and elastic. Prove for 1 hour in an oiled polythene bag.

2   Divide the dough into 20 pieces and shape into round balls. Rest for 5 minutes. Roll out each ball into long strips and either roll up like a whirl or simply leave as rounds. Make cuts on the top to form a pattern. Prove for 35 minutes or until rolls have risen. Egg wash the tops. Sprinkle with seeds.

3   Bake as above. When done, allow to cool before filling, or simply leave plain.

Secret tip: For cottage rolls, divide the dough into 50g/2oz pieces and then section off a quarter of each piece to make a small ball. Seal onto the top of the remainder of each rolls, egg wash and process as above. Try sprinkling carraway seeds or make a few cuts on the top as a pattern. A light dusting of flour gives a nice farmhouse appearance.

Serving suggestion: Salt beef, a little mustard and a slice of pickled cucumber go well inside this roll. Just the thing to eat at supper!

Freezing: Up to 3 months.

Easter Buns

Makes 24   Preparation time: 2½hours   Baking time: 20 minutes

After a cold, depressing winter we celebrate spring with large numbers of Hot Cross Buns, filled with spicy currants and mixed orange and lemon peel.

For the buns:
550g/1lb 4oz strong white flour
1 tablespoon milk powder
1 teaspoon salt
75g/3oz magarine
75g/3oz sugar
1 large egg
40g/1½oz yeast
275ml/10fl oz warm water
100g/4oz sultanas
100g/4oz currants
25g/1oz mixed peel
Zest and juice of an orange and
  lemon
25g/1oz mixed spice
½ teaspoon vanilla essence

For the 'Hot Cross':
100g/4oz soft plain flour
Pinch salt
Pinch baking powder
25g/1oz oil
100ml/4fl oz cold water

For the syrup:
225g/8oz sugar
150ml/5fl oz boiled water
Zests of orange and lemon
1 tablespoon rum

Use 2 ×30cm/12in baking sheets, well oiled

Pre-heat the oven to 230°C/450°F/Gas Mark 8
Microwave: 2 minutes on low setting and then transfer to the conventional oven to bake completely for 5 minutes until brown.

1   Blend together the flour, milk powder and salt. Cream the margarine and sugar together and add the egg. Stir well and add to the dry ingredients.

2   Dissolve the yeast in the warm water and add to the above mixture. Mix well and knead until the dough is smooth and elastic.

3   Mix all the fruits, spices and vanilla together. Disperse throughout the dough. Prove in an oiled polythene bag for 1 hour.

4   Divide the dough into 24 buns, mould into rounds and place on the baking sheets. Return to the bag and prove for a further 40 minutes until well risen.

5   For the 'Hot Cross' topping, mix the flour, salt, baking powder and oil. Add the water and stir to a piping consistency. Pipe crosses on the tops of the buns. Bake as above.

6   To make the syrup, dissolve the sugar in the water and add the zest and rum. When the buns are baked, glaze the tops while still hot.

Secret tip: Pipe different designs as an alternative to the crosses. This dough will make very good fruit loaves. For a better flavour, mix the spice with the fruit and leave overnight.

Serving suggestion: Just toast in front of the fire with butter and jam on Good Friday, and feel the glow spreading from head to toe.

Freezing: This dough will keep for up to 1 month.

Spiced Boston Tea Bread

Makes 4 loaves   Preparation time: 2 hours   Baking time: 30 minutes

On long hot summer afternoons enjoy this tea bread under a shady tree with all the family.

For the tea bread:
900g/2lb strong white flour
1 tablespoon milk powder
2 teaspoons salt
50g/2oz margarine
50g/2oz sugar
40g/1½oz yeast
575ml/1 pint warm water
275g/10oz sultanas
*Zest and juice of orange and
   lemon*
2 teaspoons cinnamon
1 teaspoon mixed spice

For the syrup:
225g/8oz sugar
150ml/5fl oz boiled water
Zest of orange and lemon
1 tablespoon rum

Use 4 × 450g/1lb loaf tins, well oiled

Pre-heat the oven to 220°C/425°F/Gas Mark 7
Microwave: Not recommended. Transfer to a conventional oven.

---

1   Blend together the flour, milk powder and salt. Cream the margarine and sugar together. Add to the above dry ingredients.

2   Dissolve the yeast in warm water and add to the above. Mix well and knead until smooth and elastic.

3   Mix all the fruits and spice together. Disperse throughout the dough. Prove in an oiled polythene bag for 1 hour.

4   Divide the dough into 4 loaves. Mould round and shape into long loaf. Place into the tins. Return to oiled polythene bags and prove for 40 minutes until well risen. Bake until golden brown (30 minutes or so).

5   To make the syrup, dissolve the sugar in the water and add the zest and rum. When baked, glaze the tops of the loaves while still hot.

Secret tip: This dough makes good fruit buns. For a better flavour, mix the spice with the fruit and leave overnight.

Serving suggestion: Spread slices with peanut butter and serve up to the hungry at teatime.

Freezing: This loaf could keep for up to 1 month.

Barrimore Barm Brack

Makes 4 loaves   Preparation time: 2½ hours   Baking time: 30 minutes

We used to travel miles along dusty country tracks to get to Caitlin's house in Ireland but she always made us welcome with her favourite bread. A light speckled loaf with a hint of blarney.

For the starter dough:
275ml/½ pint warm water
1 tablespoon sugar
25g/1oz yeast
50g/2oz strong white flour

For the dough:
450g/1lb strong white flour
1 teaspoon salt
40g/1½oz sugar
75g/3oz lard or margarine
1 egg
675g/1lb 8oz sultanas
75g/3oz mixed peel
Zest and juice of an orange or
  lemon
1 teaspoon mixed spice

For the syrup:
225g/8oz sugar
150ml/5fl oz boiled water
Zest of a lemon or orange
1 tablespoon Irish whiskey

Use 4 × 450g/1lb round loaf tins, well oiled

Pre-heat the oven to 220°C/425°/Gas Mark 7
Microwave: Not recommended. Transfer to a conventional oven.

---

1 To make the starter dough, take the warm water and dissolve the sugar in it with the yeast and flour. Leave to rise in a warm place.

---

2 Blend together the flour and salt. Cream the sugar with the margarine. Add the egg and mix all together with the starter dough. Knead until smooth and elastic.

3 Mix all the fruits and spice together including the orange or lemon zest or juice. Disperse throughout the dough. Prove in an oiled polythene bag for 1 hour.

4 Divide the dough into 4 loaves. Mould into rounds and shape into a round loaf. Place into tins. Return to polythene bags and prove for a further 40 minutes until well risen. Bake until golden brown.

5 To make the syrup, dissolve the sugar in the water. Add the zest and whiskey. When baked, glaze the tops of the loaves while still hot.

Secret tip: A little carraway seed added to the dough will impart a distinctive flavour.

Serving suggestion: Spread slices with Irish butter and lashings of bilberry preserve. Top of the morning!

Freezing: This loaf could keep for up to 1 month.

English Butt-Chess

Makes 2 loaves   Preparation time: 2½ hours   Baking time: 30 minutes

A similar bread to the French Brioche which is enriched with eggs and butter. It makes eating toast a treat. The name is my own invention incorporating the elements of butter ('Butt') and Brioche ('Chess').

For the bread:
550g/1lb 4oz strong white flour
1 teaspoon salt
1 tablespoon milk powder
225ml/8fl oz cool water
75g/3oz sugar
25g/1oz yeast
1 teaspoon malt extract
1 large egg
100g/4oz butter

For the glaze:
2 tablespoons milk
1 egg

Use 2 × 450g/1lb round loaf tins, well oiled

Pre-heat the oven to 220°C/425°F/Gas Mark 7
Microwave: Not recommended. Transfer to a conventional oven.

---

1 Blend together the flour, salt and milk powder.

---

2 Into the water dissolve the sugar, yeast, malt extract and egg. Add to the above and mix to a dough.

---

3 Cream the butter and add to the dough. Mix all together well until smooth and elastic. Leave to rise in a warm place for 2 hours.

---

4 Divide the dough into 2 loaves, mould into round loaf-shapes and place into the tins. Egg wash the dough and make 2 cuts in the shape of a cross on the tops. Return to an oiled polythene bag for 40 minutes to prove until well risen. Bake until golden brown.

Secret tip: Scale the dough into 40g/1½oz pieces, as an alternative, and then mould into rounds. Place into greased patty tins and bake as above. Also, after making the dough, leave it in the fridge overnight as this will improve the texture and flavour.

Serving suggestion: As a breakfast treat, eat three Butt-Chess with ample helpings of maple syrup, a filtered cup of Continental coffee and you're set for the day!

Freezing: This loaf will keep for 3 months.

Conil's 7-till-11 loaf

Makes 6 loaves   Preparation time: 2½ hours   Baking time: 30 minutes

This is an any-time sweet bread which is soft and fruity with a buttery flavour. Not easy to make, but well worth trying.

For the pre-dough:
225g/8oz strong white flour
25g/1oz milk powder
25g/1oz sugar
40g/1½oz yeast
150ml/ ¼ pint warm water

For the dough:
575ml/1 pint eggs, beaten
1 teaspoon salt
50g/2oz sugar
675g/1lb 8oz strong white flour

For the filling:
450g/1lb butter, melted
150g/5oz sultanas
100g/4oz apples, chopped
50g/2oz apricots, soaked
100g/4oz sugar
25g/1oz cinnamon
Sugar Syrup (page 183)

For the glaze:
2 tablespoons milk
1 egg

For decoration:
Almonds, flaked

Use 6 × 15 cm/6in (diameter) 6.5cm/2½in (depth) round tins, well oiled.

Pre-heat the oven to 220°C/425°F/Gas Mark 7
Microwave: Not recommended. Use a conventional oven.

1 For the pre-dough blend together the flour, milk powder and sugar. Dissolve the yeast in the water and add to the dry ingredients. Mix to a dough. Prove for 30 minutes.

2   For the dough, blend together the beaten egg, salt, sugar and flour. Add to the above and mix to a smooth, elastic dough. Rest for 30 minutes.

3   Divide the dough in half. Line the tins with one half to a thickness of 5mm/¼in and roll the other half flat. Spread the melted butter over this. Mix the fruits, sugar and cinnamon together. Sprinkle over the top of the flat dough, and turn over into a Swiss-roll.

4   Cut into slices and place on buttered dough-lined tins, 5 to each tin. Egg wash and then place all the tins into polythene bags which have been oiled. Leave to prove for 40 minutes until well risen. Bake until golden brown (approximately 30 minutes). When baked, glaze with the syrup and sprinkle with flaked almonds.

Secret tip: Instead of cutting the Swiss-roll into slices, cut it lengthwise to form two pieces. They can be plaited together. Join ends to form a ring. Glaze with butter and prove. Bake on a 30cm/12in baking sheet. Glaze with syrup and add flaked almonds as before.

Serving suggestion: Best on its own with a cup of lemon tea.

Freezing: Up to 3 months.

Festive Stollen

Makes 3 loaves   Preparation time: 2½ hours   Baking time: 30 minutes

Whilst working in a famous pâtisserie in London, it was my job to make the Stollen — not one but hundreds! I remember Hans, the foreman, telling me, 'Always put plenty of fruit and almond paste in, plus a little care, to make the finest Stollen seen anywhere!' Here we go...

For the pre-dough:
25g/1oz strong white flour
1 tablespoon sugar
25g/1oz yeast
275ml/10 fl oz water

For the dough:
1 egg
75g/3oz sugar
1 teaspoon salt
500g/1lb 2oz strong white flour
1 teaspoon cinnamon
225g/8oz raisins
25g/1oz rum
100g/4oz butter
175g/6oz marzipan

For the glaze:
Sugar Syrup (page 183)
2 tablespoons milk
1 egg

To decorate:
Almonds, flaked
Icing sugar

Use 2 × 30cm/12in baking sheets, well oiled

Pre-heat the oven to 220°C/425°F/Gas Mark 7
Microwave: For 3 minutes. Transfer to a conventional oven and bake completely for 15 minutes until brown.

---

1   For the pre-dough, blend together the flour and sugar. Dissolve the yeast in water and leave for 30 minutes.

2 Add to the above the egg, sugar, salt and flour. Mix to a smooth, elastic dough. Add the spice, raisins, rum and mix in well. Rest for 30 minutes.

3 Divide the dough into 3, shape into rounds and roll each out flat. Spread a little melted butter over the top. Roll out the marzipan and place in the centre of each round. Turn over the edges of each one, and press down in the centre to form a flan case effect. Place on a baking sheet.

4 Egg wash and place in oiled polythene bags to prove for 40 minutes until well risen. Bake until golden brown. When baked, glaze with syrup and sprinkle the tops with flaked almonds and icing sugar.

Secret tip: As an alternative, shape into rounds roll flat, divide into 8 prove and bake as before. The marzipan can be shaped into patterns and put on each section after baking.

Serving suggestion: At Christmas, Stollen can be served after dinner with a glass of old port.

Freezing: Up to 3 months.

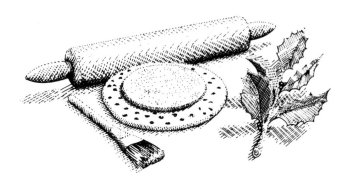

Sylvia's Savarins and Babas

Makes 20   Preparation time: 2½ hours   Baking time: 25 minutes

My father's favourite dessert — secretly soaking the savarins in a syrupy rum mixture, he would say it brought out the real flavour. It can be addictive!

For the dough:
450g/1lb strong white flour
½ teaspoon salt
1 tablespoon sugar
275ml/½ pint eggs, beaten
25g/1oz yeast
50g/2fl oz water
175g/6oz butter, melted
Sugar Syrup (page 183)

For the babas:
100g/4oz currants

Use 20 savarin/baba patty pan moulds, well oiled

Pre-heat the oven to 230°C/450°F/Gas Mark 8
Microwave: Not recommended unless baked in special microwave containers. Transfer to the conventional oven.

1   Blend together the flour, salt and sugar. Add the eggs and dissolve the yeast in the water. Mix together to form a smooth dough and leave for 1 hour till risen.

2   To this dough, add the melted butter. Mix to a soft elastic dough. For the babas, add the currants at this point. Mix well. Rest for 10 minutes.

3   Using a 1cm/½in plain tube, pipe the mixture into the moulds until each mould is half full. For babas use dariol pans.

4   Prove for 40 minutes or until well risen. Bake until golden brown. When baked, soak each in the syrup. Drain well.

Secret tip: Use any liqueur to soak the savarins — kirsch, Cointreau, etc. Make sure the syrup is boiled for best results.

Serving suggestion: For a special dessert, glaze the tops with boiled apricot jam and decorate with a mixture of fresh fruits, a dash of kirsch and top with fresh cream.

Freezing: Unsoaked, these will keep for 3 months.

Basic Bun Dough

Makes 16 buns   Preparation time: 2½ hours   Baking time: 20 minutes

For a variety of different types of buns, use this recipe. It will produce light, soft dough for anything from Swiss to Hot Cross Buns.

For the dough:
500g/1lb 2oz strong white flour
½ teaspoon salt
2 tablespoons sugar
50g/2oz butter
25g/1oz yeast (approximately)
150ml/5fl oz milk
150ml/5fl oz water
1 teaspoon vanilla essence
Sugar Syrup (page 183)

Use 2 × 30cm/12in baking sheets, well oiled

Pre-heat the oven to 230°C/450°F/Gas Mark 8
Microwave: Not recommended unless baked in special microwave containers. Transfer to a conventional oven.

---

1   Blend together the flour, salt, sugar and butter. Dissolve the yeast in the milk and water and add to the above. Add the vanilla essence. Mix to a smooth dough. Leave for 1 hour until risen.

---

2   Divide the dough into 16 pieces and shape into round balls or fingers. Place onto the baking sheets, well spaced. Prove for 40 minutes or until dough has risen.

---

3   Bake as above. When baked, glaze with syrup.

Secret tip: For Swiss Buns, ice the tops. Belgian Buns are similar — just ice the top and place a cherry in the middle. As this is a rich dough, you may need a little more yeast than stated.

Serving suggestion: Place on a plate and watch them vanish as the children arrive home.

Freezing: Un-iced will keep for 3 months.

Hazelburg Fingers

Makes 20 buns   Preparation time: 2½ hours   Baking time: 20 minutes

One of the variations using the Basic Bun Dough with the addition of hazelnuts and ginger.

For the fingers:
1kg/2lb Basic Bun Dough
  (page 57)
100g/4oz butter, melted
100g/4oz hazelnuts, ground
50g/2oz stem ginger, chopped
1 teaspoon cinnamon
½ teaspoon nutmeg

For the topping:
50g/2oz Sugar Syrup (page 183)
  and water
75g/3oz hazelnuts, flaked

Use 2 × 30cm/12in baking sheets, well oiled

Pre-heat the oven to 220°C/425°F/Gas Mark 7
Microwave: Not recommended unless baked in special microwave containers. Transfer to a conventional oven.

---

1 Roll out the dough to a rectangle approximately 30cm/12in × 50cm/20in. Spread with melted butter and then sprinkle with ground hazelnuts, ginger and spices.

2 Fold the plain side over two-thirds, and then fold it back on itself to form three layers of dough. Cut into 1cm/½in strips. Twist them to form a 'rope' effect. Place onto the baking sheets, well spaced out. Prove for 35 minutes or until the dough has risen. Bake for 15—20 minutes till brown When baked, glaze with the syrup thinned with a little water and dip into roasted flaked hazelnuts.

Secret tip: Replace the hazelnuts with almonds and ginger with raisins for a different taste. Just ice the top and place a cherry in the centre.

Serving suggestion: Makes an ideal snack with a cup of fresh ground coffee.

Freezing: Un-iced, these buns will keep for 3 months.

Glastonbury Lardy

Makes 3 loaves   Preparation time: 2½ hours   Baking time: 30 minutes

Before the days of diets, lard was used extensively in baking. Lardy is a rich bread with a velvety texture and plenty of natural goodness — a meal on its own.

For the lardy:
1kg/2lb Basic Bun Dough
  (page 57)
150g/5oz lard or butter, creamed
75g/3oz caster sugar
100g/4oz currants
100g/4oz sultanas
50g/2oz mixed peel, chopped
½ teaspoon nutmeg

Topping:
50g/2oz lard, melted
or
50g/2oz Sugar Syrup (page 183)

Use 3 × 16.5cm/6½in round patty tins, well oiled

Pre-heat the oven to 220°C/425°F/Gas Mark 7
Microwave: Approximately 12 minutes, baked in special microwave containers.

---

1 Roll out the dough to a large rectangle (30cm/12in × 50cm/20in). Spread lard or butter over the surface and then sprinkle with sugar, fruits and spices.

---

2 Divide into 3 equal parts. Fold each piece over to form a three-layer cake. Shape each piece to fit the tins. The dough should be fairly sticky. Prove for 45 minutes or until the dough has risen. (Note that because of the high fat content, it will take longer to prove than other doughs.)

---

3 Bake for 30 minutes till completely brown. When baked and still hot, glaze with melted lard or syrup.

Secret tip: A quick method is to chop the dough, lard, fruit and spice together. Divide it into 3 and place into well greased tins. Prove as above.

Serving suggestion: Serve hot on a cold wintry day with a glass of spicy mulled wine. Count calories in the spring!

Freezing: Un-iced will keep for 3 months.

Chocolate Almond Plait

Makes 2 plaits   Preparation time: 2½ hours   Baking time: 20—25 minutes

The combination of chocolate and almonds makes this a favourite choice of tea bread at any time. One slice leads to another.

For the plaits:
1kg/2lb Basic Bun Dough
  (page 57)
225g/8oz marzipan
275g/10oz brown sugar
275g/10oz butter
1 egg
50g/2oz cocoa powder
100g/4oz almonds, chopped

½ teaspoon cinnamon
3 tablespoons milk and egg

For the topping:
100g/4oz apricot jam
100g/4oz Sugar Syrup (page 183)
50g/2oz almonds, flaked

Use 2 × 30cm/12in baking sheets, well oiled

Pre-heat the oven to 220°C/425°F/Gas Mark 7
Microwave: Approximately 10 minutes, baked on special microwave ware.

1 Roll out the dough to a large rectangle (30cm/12in × 60cm/24in).

2 Cream the marzipan, sugar and butter to a light consistency. Add the egg and beat well in. Blend in the cocoa, almonds and cinnamon to make a batter. Spread the batter down the centre of the dough leaving a 7.5cm/3in border.

3 At an angle, cut along the border to a depth of 2cm/¾in. Wet the edges and from the top, fold the strips over like a plait until covered. Egg wash. Cut into 2 pieces.

4 Place on to a baking sheet allowing room for expansion. Prove for 35 minutes or until the plaits have risen. Bake in a moderate oven for 20—25 minutes until brown. When baked and whilst still hot, glaze with bottled apricot jam and syrup. Sprinkle with the flaked almonds.

Secret tip: An alternative filling can be made by substituting coffee for the cocoa and almonds. Add chopped walnuts and a touch of rum too.

Serving suggestion: Cut into thin slices and serve with a glass of dry sherry.

Freezing: Will keep for 3 months.

Old Chelsea Buns

Makes 24 buns   Preparation time: 2½ hours   Baking time: 15—20 minutes

During the seventeenth century a much-frequented place was the Olde Bunne House in Chelsea. Crowds used to gather outside to taste the famous square and spicy delicacy. With the addition of dates, the recipe remains the same. Watch out for the crowds!

For the buns:
1kg/2lb Basic Bun Dough
  (page 57)
100g/4oz butter or lard, creamed
75g/3oz brown sugar
150g/5oz currants
50g/2oz dates, chopped
50g/2oz lemon peel, chopped
½ teaspoon cinnamon
Butter, melted

For the topping:
50g/2oz Sugar Syrup (page 183)
50g/2oz caster sugar

Use 2 × 30cm/12in long 2.5cm/1in deep baking sheets, well oiled

Pre-heat the oven to 220°C/425°F/Gas Mark 7
Microwave: Approximately 8 minutes baked on special microwave ware.

---

1   Roll out the dough to a large rectangle (30cm/12in × 50cm/20in). Spread with butter and then sprinkle with sugar, fruits and spice.

---

2   Fold over the dough Swiss-roll fashion and cut 2.5cm/1in slices. Glaze with a little melted butter. Place onto baking sheets 2.5cm/1in apart to allow for expansion. Prove for 35 minutes or until buns have risen.

---

3   Bake as above. When baked and still hot, glaze with melted butter or syrup. Dust with caster sugar.

Secret tip: Instead of slices, shape the rolled piece into circles or rings. Place into greased ring moulds. Score the top with scissors to form a pattern. Prove and bake as before.

Serving suggestion: Chelsea Buns cut in half and spread with rum or brandy butter will tempt any historian!

Freezing: Will keep for 3 months.

Portland Nut Roulade

Makes 3 loaves   Preparation time: 2½ hours   Baking time: 20—25 minutes

This loaf is very nutritious and will appeal to those who like nuts and seeds. The roulade filling is effectively displayed when it is cut into slices.

For the roulade:
1kg/2lb Basic Bun Dough
  (page 57)
175g/6oz butter
75g/3oz brown sugar
50g/2oz almonds, ground
50g/2oz hazelnuts, ground
75g/3oz mixed nuts, chopped
  (choose from almonds,
  hazelnuts, walnuts,
  peanuts, etc)
50g/2oz mixed seeds (sesame,
sunflower, pumpkin, poppy or
  carraway)
100g/4oz currants
½ teaspoon cinnamon
50g/2oz sesame seeds
3 tablespoons milk and egg

For the topping:
100g/4oz Sugar Syrup (page 183)

Use 3 × 450g/1lb loaf tins, well oiled

Pre-heat the oven to 220°C/425°F/Gas Mark 7
Microwave: Approximately 12 minutes, baked in special microwave containers.

---

1   Roll out dough to a rectangle (30cm/12in × 60cm/24in).

---

2   Cream the butter and sugar and blend in the ground almonds and hazelnuts to make a paste. Spread paste over the surface and sprinkle with the mixed nuts, seeds, currants and cinnamon.

---

3   Roll up into a long roulade and divide into 3 pieces. Place into greased loaf tins, egg wash and sprinkle with sesame seeds.

---

4   Place into baking tins and prove for 35 minutes or until loaves have risen.

---

5   Bake for 20—25 minutes till brown. Then, still hot, glaze with boiled syrup.

Secret tip: As an alternative omit the nuts and seeds and replace with cherry pie filling or cooked, chopped apples. Use sultanas instead of currants.

Serving suggestion: Serve in slices as a nice accompaniment to cream cheese.

Freezing: Up to 3 months.

Earl's Ears

Makes 24   Preparation time: 2 hours   Baking time: 20 minutes

A pagan ritual once offered pigs' ears to the Gods, the hope being that the Gods would hear the supplicants' plea and save them from the ravages of famine. Now every year, following this custom, the ears are made instead with a rich, filled dough. Let's hope the Gods are kind to us!

For the bread:
1kg/2lb Basic Bun dough
  (page 57)
100g/4oz butter, melted

For the filling:
100g/4oz butter
100g/4oz sugar
2 eggs
175g/6oz cake crumbs

50g/2oz sultanas
25g/1oz sesame or poppy seeds
¼ teaspoon aniseed
¼ teaspoon ginger
½ teaspoon mixed spice

For the topping:
100g/4oz Sugar Syrup (page 183)

Use 2 × 30cm/12in baking sheets, well oiled

Pre-heat the oven to 220°C/425°F/Gas Mark 7
Microwave: Approximately 10 minutes baked on special microwave ware.

---

1   For the filling, cream the butter and sugar lightly together, beat in the eggs and blend together with the cake crumbs, seeds and spices.

---

2   Divide the dough into 24 pieces. Shape into balls and roll flat. Spread melted butter over the surface. Spoon a portion of the filling on to each circle. Fold over the edges to form a triangle. Leave the filling showing. Glaze with the butter.

---

3   Place on to baking sheets and bake for 20 minutes until brown. When ready and still hot, glaze with boiled syrup.

Secret tip: When using poppy seeds, add a tablespoon of honey and reduce the sugar by 25g/1oz. Substitute the cake crumbs with ground almonds for a richer flavour.

Serving suggestion: Serve during the autumn with cups of hot steamy chocolate and therein dunk your Earl's Ears!

Freezing: Will keep for 3 months.

Rough and Tumble Loaf

Makes 3 loaves   Preparation time: 1½ hours   Baking time: 20—25 minutes

A very quick way to produce a delicious fruity bread; its 'rough' appearance gives this loaf its appeal.

For the bread:
1kg/2lb Basic Bun Dough
  (page 57)
175g/6oz sultanas
75g/3oz mixed peel
50g/2oz cherries, chopped
50g/2oz angelica, chopped
75g/3oz nibbed sugar (coarse)
2 eggs
½ teaspoon mixed spice
3 tablespoons egg and milk

For the topping:
100g/4oz Sugar Syrup (page 183)
50g/2oz nibbed sugar

Use 3 × 450g/1lb loaf tins, well oiled

Pre-heat the oven to 220°C/425°F/Gas Mark 7
Microwave: Approximately 12 minutes, baked in special microwave containers.

---

1   In a large bowl put the dough, fruits, sugar, eggs and spice. Using a flat metal scraper, chop the mixture until all the ingredients are combined. Leave fairly rough.

---

2   Divide the mixture into 3 pieces and place them into greased loaf tins. Egg wash and sprinkle with nibbed sugar.

---

3   Prove for 35 minutes or until the loaves have risen. Bake in a moderate oven for 20—25 minutes. When baked and still hot, glaze with boiled syrup.

Secret tip: Do not overmix. Add walnuts instead of peel to give a nutty flavour.

Serving suggestion: Serve sliced with butter and pineapple preserve, a cup of Earl Grey tea and a good book to while away the afternoon!

Freezing: Up to 3 months.

Taunton Cheese Slice

Makes 2   Preparation time: 2 hours   Baking time: 35 minutes

Cheesecake has always been my favourite — the sharp sweetness and smooth texture mingled with choice fruits is the main ingredient in this recipe. Any fruits can be added — I've used chopped apples.

For the bread:
450g/1lb Basic Bun Dough
  (page 57)

For the filling:
500g/1lb 2oz curd cheese
175g/6oz sugar
1 egg
75g/3oz fresh cream, whipped
75g/3oz flour

75g/3oz butter, melted
225g/8oz apples, chopped and
  cooked
100g/4oz sultanas
½ teaspoon cinnamon

For the topping:
50g/2oz butter, melted
100g/4oz Sugar Syrup (page 183)

Use a 30cm/12in baking sheet, well oiled

Pre-heat the oven to 200°C/400°F/Gas Mark 6
Microwave: Approximately 12 minutes baked on special microwave ware.

---

1 To make the filling, lightly cream the curd cheese and sugar and beat in the egg. Blend in the cream and flour together and pour on the melted butter. Add the apples with the sultanas and cinnamon. Mix well.

---

2 Roll out the dough to a square (30cm/12in by 30cm/12in). Cut it in half and wet the edges. Down the centre of one half spread the filling and place the other half of the dough on top. Pinch the edges to seal. Make cuts diagonally to expose the cheese filling. Spread melted butter over the surface.

---

3 Place on to baking sheet and prove for 35 minutes or till the slices have risen.

---

4 Bake for 35 minutes until brown and set. When baked and still hot, glaze with boiled syrup.

Secret tip: As an alternative, spread the filling over the surface of the dough. Add pistachio nuts instead of fruit and roll up Swiss-roll fashion. Continue as above.

Serving suggestion: Cut into slices and serve as a dessert.

Freezing: Up to 3 months.

Royal Bath Buns

Makes 24   Preparation time: 2 hours   Baking time: 15—20 minutes

Having missed the last train back to college one evening, I was forced to seek refreshment in the railway buffet. A plate of Bath Buns looked inviting and soon disappeared as the day dawned. When travelling, make sure you take ample supplies — they could make all the difference.

For the pre-mix:
150ml/5fl oz warm milk
1 tablespoon sugar
20g/3/4oz yeast
50g/2oz flour

For the dough:
450g/1lb strong white flour
175g/6oz butter
2 eggs
225g/8oz nibbed sugar (coarse)
75g/3oz sultanas
50g/2oz citron peel, chopped
25g/1oz orange peel, chopped
1 zest lemon or orange
½ teaspoon nutmeg

For the topping:
1 egg
50g/2oz nibbed sugar
100g/4oz Sugar Syrup (page 183)

Use 2 × 30cm/12in baking sheets, well oiled

Pre-heat the oven to 220°C/425°F/Gas Mark 7
Microwave: Approximately 8 minutes baked on special microwave ware.

---

1   To make the pre-mix, dissolve in the milk the sugar, yeast and flour. Mix well and leave till risen (approximately 30 minutes).

---

2   Blend together the flour, butter and eggs and add to the above pre-mix. Knead for 10 minutes by hand, or 3 minutes in the food processor, until smooth and elastic. Prove for 1 hour in an oiled polythene bag or till double size.

3   Transfer dough to a bowl and add all the sugar, fruit and spice. Chop roughly leaving a coarse mixture. With a spoon, deposit small mounds of the mixture (50g/2oz) on the greased baking sheets allowing room to expand.

4   Prove for 35 minutes or until the buns have risen. Egg wash and sprinkle a little sugar on the top.

5   Bake for 15—20 minutes till golden brown. Whilst still hot, glaze with boiled syrup.

Secret tip: The dough can be used for a variety of buns, including Swiss Long Fingers with icing on top; doughnuts — round balls deep fried in oil and filled with jam; teacakes — a flat round bun used for toasting; fruit buns, and loaves.

Serving suggestion: These buns are even more enticing cut in half and buttered with a little lemon curd and served with a nice cup of tea.

Freezing: Uncooked will keep for 3 months.

Camborne Saffron Loaf

Makes 3 loaves   Preparation time: 2½ hours   Baking time: 30 minutes

In the nineteenth century, saffron was cultivated for its delicate flavour and strong yellow colour. Used then extensively in all types of cooking and baking, unfortunately today saffron is little used and very expensive. In this recipe only a small amount is used, so let's spoil ourselves.

For the pre-mix:
150ml/5fl oz milk
150ml/5fl oz water
1 teaspoon sugar
25g/1oz yeast
150g/5oz strong white flour

For the dough:
375g/13oz strong white flour
½ teaspoon salt
1 tablespoon sugar
150g/5oz butter
½ teaspoon filament saffron
(infused)
225g/8oz currants
100g/4oz sultanas
25g/1oz orange peel
25g/1oz walnuts, chopped
Sugar Syrup (page 183)

Use 3 × 450g/1lb loaf tins, well oiled

Pre-heat the oven to 220°C/425°F/Gas Mark 7
Microwave: Not recommended unless baked in special microwave containers. Transfer to a conventional oven.

1   For the pre-mix, mix the milk and water and dissolve the sugar, yeast and flour. Leave to rise in a warm place.

2   Blend together the flour, salt, sugar and butter. Infuse the saffron in a little water and add to the above. Mix to a smooth dough. Add the dried fruits and walnuts and mix to a smooth elastic dough. Leave for 30 minutes until risen.

68

3   Divide dough into 3 pieces and shape into long sausages. Place into well oiled tins and cut a pattern with scissors on the tops. Prove for 40 minutes till the dough is level with the lip of the tin. Bake as above. When baked, glaze with syrup.

Secret tip: Use this loaf to make bread and butter pudding. Add a sprinkling of nutmeg and bake as normal.

Serving suggestion: Cut into slices, dip into egg/milk mixture and fry in hot butter for a few minutes each side. Serve as a breakfast starter.

Freezing: Uncooked will keep for 3 months.

Canape Rolls

Makes 30   Preparation time: 2 hours   Baking time: 15—20 minutes

Always popular at parties and functions, these rolls are an ideal base for numerous fillings. A small, soft and sweet roll, these are easy to make and guaranteed to disappear when laden with savoury titbits.

For the rolls:
450g/1lb strong white flour
1 tablespoon milk powder
1 teaspoon salt
15g/½oz sugar
25g/1oz shortening

25g/1oz yeast
1 egg
275ml/½ pint warm water

For the topping:
1 egg

Use 2 × 30cm/12in baking sheets, well oiled

Pre-heat the oven to 230°C/450°F/Gas Mark 8
Microwave: Approximately 6 minutes baked on special microwave ware.

---

1   Blend together the flour, milk powder, salt and sugar. Then add the fat. Soak the yeast in the water and egg and add to the mixture. Knead for 10 minutes by hand or 3 minutes in a food processor until smooth and elastic. Prove for 1 hour in an oiled polythene bag.

---

2   Divide the dough into 30 pieces and shape into round balls. Rest for 5 minutes. Roll out each ball to the shape of a cigar or leave round as you prefer. Transfer to the baking sheets leaving room for the rolls to expand. Prove for 35 minutes or until the rolls have risen. Egg wash.

---

3   Bake for 15—20 minutes. Allow to cool before filling (see below).

Secret tip: Divide the dough into 50g/2oz pieces and mould into rounds. Cut these in half and you have the nearest thing to a Bridge Roll. Egg wash and proceed as before. Try sprinkling sesame seeds on top or make a few cuts to form a pattern.

Serving suggestion: Cut the rolls in half. Butter them and layer with a slice of parma ham, tomato, boiled egg and watercress. Use any type of meat, cheese or salad to turn canape rolls into a delicious feast.

Freezing: Up to 3 months.

CHAPTER 3
FIRESIDE, SODA AND YEAST BREADS

This chapter concentrates on soda goods which are baked without yeast. A chemical (1 part bicarbonate of soda to 2 parts cream of tartar), baking powder is used to aerate and lighten scones, crumpets and pancakes. In Ireland, bicarbonate of soda is used on its own, the acid coming from the buttermilk. The two combine together and react to produce carbon dioxide which aerates the dough during baking.

The scone dates back to the time when hot stones were used to cook these mealy morsels. These hot stones were known as a 'Greadeal', and later became known as a 'Griddle' or 'Girdle' as it is known in the North of England and Scotland. Oatmeal was used to produce many types of hot plate cakes and also the pancake as it is known today in England, which is a flat round buttercake usually served as a pudding. In Scotland these are known as pikelets and eaten as a sweetbread.

The griddle should be prepared well in advance of cooking. Heat for at least 30 minutes. Lightly grease the surface and check temperatures by lightly dusting flour onto the hot plate where it should turn brown in a few minutes. If so, it is ready to bake your scones or pancakes. Remember to turn over to brown both sides. If you prefer you can bake them in the conventional oven. Enjoy those fireside memories of long ago.

Kelly's Soda Farls

Makes 2 farls   Preparation time: 30 minutes   Baking time: 20—30 minutes

Ireland's favourite bread takes full advantage of the abundant milk available, turning buttermilk and flour into beautiful morsels with the mininum of fuss. Use sour milk or cream.

For the farls:
675g/1lb 8oz wheatmeal flour
2 teaspoons salt
100g/4oz sugar
1 tablespoon cream of tartar
25g/1oz butter
1 teaspoon bicarbonate of soda
575ml/1 pint buttermilk or milk

For the topping:
1 egg
50g/2oz wheatmeal flour

Use 2 × 30cm/12in baking sheets, well oiled

Pre-heat the oven to 230°C/450°F/Gas Mark 8
Use the hot plate as an alternative to baking. See 'Secret Tips' below.
Microwave: Approximately 3 minutes, baked on microwave ware. Transfer to the conventional oven to brown.

---

1   In a mixing bowl blend together the flour, salt, sugar and cream of tartar. Add the butter and rub in. Mix the bicarbonate of soda with the milk and stir into the dry ingredients until the dough is clear, that is, until it is smooth and even in consistency.

---

2   Transfer to a lightly floured table. Divide the dough into 2 or 3 pieces and shape into rounds. Roll out to a 2cm/¾in thickness.

---

3   Place the farls on the baking sheets allowing room for expansion. Divide them into 4 quarters by gently marking the surface of each one. Egg wash and dust with flour. Bake immediately in the hot oven for 20—30 minutes until golden brown.

Secret tips: Use baking powder instead of bicarbonate of soda and cream of tartar if these are not available. If using milk, soak half the flour in half the milk for 2 hours to produce a substitute for buttermilk. The flavour and texture is greatly improved by doing this.

Increase the milk content to make griddle or hot plate farls. Bake for 5—10 minutes on each side.

Variations: *Chopped Nuts*: Use mixed nuts roughly chopped (75g/3oz). Top with cracked wheat.
Mixed Seeds: Use sesame, sunflower, pumpkin or carraway. Add 50g/2oz to dough mixture and top with wholemeal flour.
Serve hot with mountains of Irish butter and a glass of their famous stout!

Freezing: Up to 3 months.

Countryman Scones

Makes 24   Preparation time: 1 hour   Baking time: 15—20 minutes

A quick way to make aerated bread using baking powder. One can make a variety of teatime favourites in this way. Always use milk, for the lactic acid benefits the lift and flavour of the finished product.

For the scones:
450g/1lb strong white flour
Pinch of salt
75g/3oz shortening
75g/3oz sugar
25g/1oz baking powder

275ml/½ pint milk
75g/3oz sultanas
½ teaspoon nutmeg

For the topping:
1 egg

Use 2 × 30cm/12in baking sheets, well oiled

Pre-heat the oven to 230°C/450°F/Gas Mark 8
Microwave: Approximately 6 minutes, baked on special microwave ware.

1 Blend together in a mixing bowl the flour, salt, shortening and sugar. Add the baking powder and then the milk to form a soft dough. Mix in the sultanas and spice till well distributed.

2 Transfer the scone mixture to a lightly floured table. Roll out to 1cm/½in thickness. Use a 6cm/2¼in cutter to cut out the scones. Use all the dough.

3 Place the scones on the baking sheets allowing room for expansion. Egg wash the tops and rest for 10 minutes before baking in a hot oven for 15—20 minutes until golden brown.

Variations: *'Farmhouse':* Dust with flour before baking.
Desiccated Coconut: Add 25g/1oz of coconut instead of sultanas. Dip the tops in coconut before baking.
Fruit: Use mixed peel, glacé cherries or currants (50g/2oz) instead of the sultanas.
Choc-chip: Add 50g/2oz chocolate chips plus a pinch of cinnamon.
Grated Cheese: Add 75g/3oz grated cheese, omit the sugar and sprinkle sesame seeds on top.
Devonshire Splits: Cut the plain scones and add cream and jam. Dust with icing sugar.

Freezing: Will keep for up to 3 months.

Oaties

Makes 5   Preparation time: 30 minutes
Baking time: 25—30 minutes or hot plate: 5—10 minutes

Traditionally of Celtic origin where the harsh climate of the northern lands lends itself to the wholesome body warming glow of these oat cakes, oaties are best when baked on the griddle.

For the oaties:
400g/14oz oatmeal
50g/2oz wholemeal flour
Pinch of salt
50g/2oz butter
15g/½oz bicarbonate of soda
275ml/½ pint water or milk

Use 2 × 30cm/12in baking sheets, well oiled

Pre-heat the oven to 190°C/375°F/Gas Mark 5
Use a hot plate for best results as an alternative to baking.
Microwave: Approximately 3 minutes, baked on microwave ware.

1   Blend together the oatmeal, the flour and the salt. Rub in the butter. Mix the bicarbonate of soda with the water or milk and stir into the dry ingredients until the dough is clear.

2   Transfer the mixture to a lightly floured table and divide into 4—5 pieces. Shape into rounds and roll out flat. Place the oaties on the baking sheets allowing room for expansion. Lightly mark them into quarters and dust with flour. Bake immediately in a low oven for 25—30 minutes till dried or use the griddle. The oaties are ready when the ends curl up.

Secret tip: Take care with baking. They should be completely dry. For a rougher texture, add 50g/2oz rolled oats instead of the flour.

Variations: *Chopped Nuts*:   Use any nuts (75g/3oz).
Mixed Seeds: Use sesame, sunflower, pumpkin or carraway seeds, adding 50g/2oz to the dough.

Serving suggestion: Serve hot with eggs and bacon or as an accompaniment to Cock-a-leekie Soup.

Freezing: Will freeze for 3 months or keep for several weeks in an airtight tin.

Scotch Pikelets

Makes 24   Preparation time: 30 minutes   Baking time: 5—10 minutes

The griddle was used extensively before modern appliances were introduced. In one variation, a flat iron was lowered onto the fire to heat up. The batters were then spooned on and turned to produce golden coloured discs of delight. Pikelets are best when baked on the griddle or hot iron.

For the pikelets:
450g/1lb strong white flour
Pinch of baking powder
Pinch of salt
25g/1oz butter, melted
150g/5oz sugar
1 egg
400ml/¾ pint milk
75g/3oz currants

Use a griddle or hot plate, well oiled

Microwave: Not recommended. Using hot plate for best results (or a frying pan if necessary) is essential.

1   Blend together the flour, baking powder and salt. Melt the butter and add the sugar, egg and milk. Mix well. Add to the dry ingredients. Mix to a batter.

2   Using a spoon, deposit the mixture on to a hot griddle, giving pikelets which are approximately 5cm/2in wide. Sprinkle currants into the centre of each one. When dry turn over to complete.

3   Place the pikelets on a wire tray to cool or eat straight away.

Variations: *Nuts*: Chopped, mixed nuts can be added (75g/3oz).
Mixed Seeds: Use sesame, pumpkin, carraway or sunflower seeds (50g/2oz).
Orange Slices: Place them in the centre of the pikelets when griddling.
Also choose from kiwifruit, apricots, bananas and many more.

Serving suggestion: Serve hot with maple syrup and a scoop of dairy icecream, or eat them on their own at breakfast.

Freezing: Up to 3 months.

Mill House Crumpets

Makes 20   Preparation time: 45 minutes   Hot plate time: 5—10 minutes

Homemade crumpets have a unique taste, especially when baked on a fireside griddle. Use metal hoops to stop the mixture from flowing.

For the crumpets:
550g/1lb 4oz strong white flour
Pinch of cream of tartar
25g/1oz sugar
25g/1oz yeast
575ml/1 pint warm water
Pinch of salt
Pinch of bicarbonate of soda
70ml/2½ fl oz water

Use 7.5cm/3in metal hoops, well oiled
Use a griddle or hot plate, well oiled

Microwave: Not recommended. Use hot plate or a frying pan.

---

1   Blend the flour, cream of tartar and sugar together. Dissolve the yeast in the warm water and add. Mix to a batter and leave to prove till double in size.

---

2   Stir the salt and bicarbonate of soda into the water, add to the batter and mix until the batter is clear.

---

3   Using a spoon, deposit the mixture onto a hot griddle. Crumpets should be 7.5cm/3in wide. When the tops form small holes and dry out turn over for a few minutes to toast. For best results use crumpet hoops. Remove when crumpets have set.

---

4   Place the crumpets on a wire rack to cool or eat straight away.

Serving suggestion: Serve with butter or honey, or as a savoury base for poached eggs, baked beans, steamed haddock and various cheeses. Makes a delicious Welsh rarebit with a dash of Worcester sauce.

Freezing: Up to 3 months.

Potato Fennel Pankies

Makes 8   Preparation time: 30 minutes   Hot plate time: 5—10 minutes

Potatoes have always been a staple diet of country folk. Being plentiful they lend themselves to many different uses. For a change, turn them into pancakes. The fennel gives them an unusual and pleasant flavour.

For the pankies:
225g/8oz potatoes, boiled and
  mashed
175g/6oz strong white flour
½ teaspoon baking powder
½ teaspoon salt
25g/1oz butter
1 teaspoon fennel seeds
Milk to bind

Use a griddle or hot plate, well oiled

Microwave: Not recommended. Use a hot plate for best results or a frying pan as a last resort.

---

1   Blend together the mashed potato with the other ingredients to form a smooth paste. Divide this into 8 pieces and form into round flat pancakes.

---

2   Using a spatula, place the pankies onto a hot griddle. They should be 7.5cm/3in wide. Bake for 2—3 minutes each side to toast.

---

3   Place the pankies on a wire rack to cool or eat straight away.

Variations: As a change, use carraway or sesame seeds. Try a little grated cheese mixed into the potato and chopped onion instead of the fennel seeds.

Serving suggestion: Serve hot or cold with butter and slices of home-cured gammon. The pankies will also make a delicious base for chilli con carne.

Freezing: These will keep for 3 months.

Bran and Raisin Muffins

Makes 20   Preparation time: 90 minutes   Hot plate time: 5—10 minutes

In Victorian times you could hear the 'muffin man' cry 'Try my hot muffins, four a penny', his bell ringing in the distance. Alas, those days are gone but the muffin still remains. A soft-centred honeycombed texture, these will melt in the mouth when toasted.

For the muffins:
500g/1lb 2oz wheatmeal flour
1 teaspoon salt
15g/½oz sugar
15g/½oz butter

1 egg
20g/¾oz yeast
350ml/12fl oz water
173g/6oz raisins
25g/1oz wheat bran

Use a griddle or hot plate, well oiled. Can be part-baked and then finished off on the hot plate.

Microwave: Not recommended. Use hot plate or frying pan.

---

1   Blend together in a mixing bowl the flour, salt, sugar, butter and egg. Soak the yeast in the water and add to the mixture. Mix the dough until soft and elastic. Add the fruit and disperse will. Prove for 1 hour or till well risen.

2   Divide into 20 pieces. Form them into round rolls and slightly flatten. Dip both sides into the bran.

3   Transfer each to a warm place and cover to avoid drying out. Allow to rise before placing on the hot griddle for 5—6 minutes to brown on each side. They should be 7.5cm/3in wide and the middle should be soft.

---

4   Place the finished muffins on a wire rack to cool or eat immediately.

Variations: Use white flour and omit the fruit for an authentic muffin. Add nuts seeds, dates or any other fruit.

Serving suggestion: Serve hot or cold with butter. Return to the griddle till the butter melts and then serve. Makes a delicious base for snacks.

Freezing: Will keep for 3 months.

Elizabethan Fritters

Makes 24   Preparation time: 1½ hours   Frying time: 5—6 minutes

On May Day people would gather in the Market Square with the maypole the centre of attraction. From the many stalls selling all manner of country foods, the aroma of Elizabethan Fritters would linger on the air. They were always popular with children and still are!

For the fritters:
550g/1lb 4oz strong white flour
Pinch of salt
15g/½oz sugar
40g/1½oz butter
25g/1oz yeast
400ml/14oz milk
225g/8oz currants
Zest of a lemon or orange

Deep fry at a temperature of 190°C/375°F

Microwave: Not recommended.

---

1   Blend together the flour, salt, sugar and butter. Soak the yeast in the milk and add to the dry ingredients. Mix the batter until soft, clear of lumps and elastic. Add the fruit and disperse well. Prove for 1 hour or till well risen.

---

2   Knockback and divide into 24 pieces. Form these into round rolls and drop into the hot fat to fry until golden brown.

---

3   Place the fritters on a wire rack to cool or eat straight away, tossed in caster sugar with a pinch of cinnamon.

Variations: Add chopped nuts, seeds or any dried fruit.

Serving suggestion: Serve hot or cold as a snack or dessert. Dip in chocolate sauce and sprinkle on top some toasted, flaked almonds.

Freezing: Will keep for up to 1 month.

Waffles

Makes 10   Preparation time: 30 minutes   Waffling time: 5—8 minutes

Very popular on the Continent, waffles are easy to make and go well with any fruit or syrup.

For the waffles:
450g/1lb white flour
Pinch of salt
100g/4oz icing sugar
1 teaspoon baking powder
1 egg
400ml/14fl oz milk
100g/4oz butter, melted

Use a waffle iron, pre-heated

Microwave: Not recommended.

---

1   Blend together the flour, salt, sugar and baking powder. Add the egg and the milk. Beat together well to form a batter. Pour in the melted butter and mix till clear.

---

2   For best results leave to stand for 2 hours. Pour the batter on to the oiled waffle iron to cover the surface. Place the lid down and cook till golden brown.

---

3   Remove from iron and place the waffles on a wire rack to cool or eat straight away with a dab of butter.

Variations: To enrich the waffle mixture, add a little cream and reduce the milk to compensate. Flavour with vanilla, lemon and almond.

Serving suggestion: Serve hot or cold as a snack or dessert. Dust with icing sugar and toast under the grill for a toffee flavour, or add a knob of butter and a spoonful of maple syrup.

Freezing: Will keep for up to 3 months.

Dartmoor Demons

Makes 20   Preparation time: 1 hour   Baking time: 15—20 minutes

Getting lost on Dartmoor is no joke. The mist tends to lure you into a false sense of security. Beware the demons!

For the demons:
450g/1lb 100% wholemeal flour
Pinch of salt
20g/¾oz baking powder
100g/4oz butter
100g/4oz sugar
1 egg
225ml/8fl oz milk

50g/2oz prunes, de-stoned,
  chopped and soaked
50g/2oz dates, chopped
Zest of an orange and lemon

For the topping:
1 egg
50g/2oz sesame seeds

Use 2 × 30cm/12in baking sheets, well oiled

Pre-heat the oven to 200°C/400°F/Gas Mark 6
Microwave: Approximately 3 minutes, baked on microwave ware. Transfer to conventional oven to brown.

---

1   Blend together in a mixing bowl the flour, salt and baking powder. Cream the butter and sugar together, mix in the egg and clear the batter. Add to the dry ingredients. Pour on the milk and mix to a smooth dough. Add the fruits and zest and disperse well.

---

2   Transfer the mixture to a lightly floured table, roll out to 1cm/½in thickness. Use a 6cm/2¼in cutter to cut out the scones. Press the edges of each one to form a dome. Make an indent in the middle, egg wash and place half a date in the centre. Sprinkle sesame seeds on the top.

---

3   Place the demons on the baking sheets allowing room for expansion and rest for 10 minutes before baking for 15—20 minutes until golden brown.

Variations: *Chopped Walnuts:*   Add 75g/3oz to the dough and top scones with cracked wheat.
Mixed Seeds: Use sesame, sunflower, pumpkin or carraway seeds. Add 50g/2oz and top with dusted wholemeal.
Glacé Cherries: Add 75g/3oz and top scones with ground hazelnuts.
Choc-Chip: Add 50g/2oz chocolate chips and a pinch of cinnamon.

Freezing: Will keep for 3 months.

Apricot Wholemeal Scones

Makes 24   Preparation time: 1 hour   Baking time: 15—20 minutes

Wholemeal flour produces scones which have a nutty flavour and, because all the grain is used, gives you the necessary fibre requirement for the day. The addition of apricots makes this an extra healthy recipe.

For the scones:
450g/1lb 100% wholemeal flour
Pinch of salt
50g/2oz shortening
50g/2oz sugar
25g/1oz baking powder
1 egg

275ml/½ pint milk
75g/3oz dried apricots, chopped
  and soaked
½ teaspoon mixed spice

For the topping:
1 egg

Use 2 × 30cm/12in baking sheets, well oiled

Pre-heat the oven to 230°C/450°F/Gas Mark 8
Microwave: Approximately 3 minutes baked on microwave ware.
Transfer to conventional oven to brown.

---

1   Blend together the flour, salt, shortening and sugar in a bowl. Add the baking powder, egg and the milk and mix well to form a soft dough. Mix in the apricots and spice and mix thoroughly till well dispersed.

---

2   Transfer the scone mixture to a lightly floured table and roll out to a thickness of 1cm/½in. Use a 6cm/2¼in cutter to cut out the scones using all the dough.

---

3   Place the scones on the baking sheets allowing room for expansion. Egg wash the tops. Rest for 10 minutes then bake for 15—20 minutes till golden brown.

Variations: *Chopped Dates:* Add 50g/2oz chopped dates instead of apricots. Dip the tops of the scones in nibbed almonds
Chopped Walnuts: Add 75g/3oz chopped walnuts and top the scones with cracked wheat.
Mixed Seeds: Use carraway, sunflower, pumpkin or sesame. Add 50g/2oz to the scone mixture and top the scones with a dusting of wholemeal flour.
Glacé Cherries: Add 75g/3oz cherries and top scones with ground hazelnuts.
Choc-Chip: 50g/2oz chocolate chips plus a pinch of cinnamon.
Dorset splits: Cut the wholemeal scones and fill with jam and cream or yoghurt. Dust with icing sugar.

Freezing: Up to 3 months.

CHAPTER 4

AFTERNOON TARTS AND PASTRIES

One of my most abiding memories is that of my Grandmother, dressed in black with a lace bonnet and apron, waiting at the farmhouse door to greet us affectionately after our tiring journey through the rural lanes of Northern France. As we entered into the coolness of the stone-flagged kitchen, the light glowed to reveal the many delicacies for which Grandmother was famed. The table was full of homemade delights — soft cheeses, freshly churned butter, slices of crusty bread, gammons with spicy glazes, potted meats and pâtés, pickles, preserves and wonderful creamy puddings that tempted and tormented. So we began our journey into Grandmother's world of simple cuisine, and the lessons I learnt then remain with me today.

In particular, it was her pastry that caught my attention — that delicious combination of butter, flour, eggs and sugar which together formed a delicious short paste which was the base for all her flans, tarts and pies.

In this chapter we will explore the many possibilities for the home-baking of pastries, tarts and pies. The basis for good biscuit-like pastry incorporates the following points:

1 The flour must have a low gluten content. Use a soft, plain or self-raising flour and add a little cornflour to avoid any toughening of the pastry.
2 Use caster sugar, as granulated tends to produce dark speckles on the baked pastry. Icing sugar will produce light, short, biscuit-like textures which are ideal for Viennese pastry.
3 Make sure you rub the fat into the flour finely. A similar method would be to cream the fat and sugar, add the egg and milk and then the flour, or cream the fat with half the flour and add the egg and milk. Then add the remaining flour. In all cases do not overmix or it may toughen.
4 Sugar added to the pastry — except that used for sweetening — will produce a natural caramelisation when baked in the oven. The more sugar is added, the deeper the colour and so the lower should be the oven temperature. Sugar also makes pastry shorter in texture, so be careful when handling and rolling out. Always rest the pastry prior to baking, as this will avoid any shrinkage during baking, and, as my Grandmother used to say, 'Light pastry needs a light touch.'

Sweet Pastry

Makes 450g/1lb pastry   Preparation time: 20 minutes
Baking time: 15—30 minutes

This pastry can be the base for hundreds of pies, tarts and pastry dishes. Who can resist the temptation of freshly-made fruit pie? The secret is in the handling. The only additive I use is TLC — tender loving care!

For the pastry:
100g/4oz butter or margarine
225g/8oz plain soft flour
1 egg
50g/2oz caster sugar
Pinch of salt

Pre-heat the oven to 190°C/375°F — 220°C/425°F — G Mark 5—7

Microwave: From 3—12 minutes

---

1   Rub in the butter and flour till fine and clear. Mix the egg with the sugar and salt. Add to the crumble mixture until pastry forms a short, pliable dough. (The 'rub-in' method)

OR

Cream the butter and sugar for a minute and then add the egg. Mix to a clear dough. Blend in the flour and salt, and form a short pliable dough (the 'cream-in' method).

Secret tip: Only use soft flour for short pastry, as strong flour will toughen the pastry, making it hard and tough to eat. To enrich the pastry, increase the butter or use water instead of the egg. For best results, keep the pastry in the fridge or freezer.
Do not overmix the pastry as it will shrink and toughen when baked.
Do not over-cream the butter and sugar, as it will become too short and difficult to pin out.

Freezing: Will keep for up to 3 months.

Apple Lime Meringue Pie

Makes 2   Preparation time: 35 minutes   Baking time: 20—30 minutes

A summer delight, the soft clouds of meringue floating on a cushion of fruity apples and limes.

For the pie:
450g/1lb Sweet Pastry (page 85)

For the filling:
25g/1oz cornflour
275ml/½ pint boiling water
75g/3oz sugar

Juice and zest of 3 limes
225g/8oz apples, cooked and chopped
50g/2oz butter
3 eggs, separated
75g/3oz sugar

Use 2 × 20cm/8in round pie dishes, well oiled

Pre-heat the oven to 200°C/400°F/Gas Mark 6
Microwave: After 6 minutes transfer to conventional oven to brown.

1   Roll out the pastry and line 2 pie dishes. Pinch the edges to form a border.

2   For the filling, dissolve the cornflour in a little cold water. Boil the remainder and add the cornflour. Continue boiling till thickened. Add the sugar, juice and zest of the limes and bring to the boil. Cool. Add the apples, butter, egg yolks and mix to clear. Pour into pastry cases and part bake for 10—15 minutes.

3   Whisk egg whites together with the sugar to a peak. Pipe onto the pie the meringue or spread with a palette knife forming peaks.

4   Bake until golden in colour (10—15 minutes).

Variations: Use lemons instead of apples and limes. Sprinkle with flaked nuts before baking. Oranges or any citrus fruit can be used.

Serving suggestion: Serve as a dessert, at picnics or any outdoor event.

Freezing: Will not freeze well. Eat as soon as possible.

Congress Tarts

Makes 12   Preparation time: 20 minutes   Baking time: 15—20 minutes

The Romans were fond of almonds and sweetmeats. These contained mixtures of honey, ground nuts and were flavoured with rose water. Today we still enjoy these nutty mixtures using egg whites to lighten the texture. A wide selection of almond pastries can be made using the basic recipe.

For the tarts:
450g/1lb Sweet Pastry (page 85)
100g/4oz raspberry jam

15g/½oz ground rice
4 medium egg whites

For the topping:
100g/4oz almonds, ground
225g/8oz caster sugar

Use 12 × 7.5cm/3in round tart pans

Pre-heat the oven to 180°C/350°F/Gas Mark 4
Microwave: After 3 minutes transfer to conventional oven to brown.

---

1   Roll out the pastry and line 12 tart pans. Trim edges and pipe a little jam into the centre of each.

---

2   For the topping, mix the almonds, sugar and rice together. Whisk the egg whites in a bowl and add the dry ingredients. Rest for 3 minutes in a food processor on a medium speed. Using a 1cm/½in plain piping tube, pipe the pans half full with almond paste.

---

3   With the leftover pastry, roll out very thin and cut strips 7.5cm/3in long. Place 2 in the form of a cross on the top of each tart.

---

4   Bake for 15—20 minutes until golden in colour.

Variations: Pipe any type of jam into the centre of each tart to suit your taste. As a contrast sprinkle rum-soaked sultanas inside instead of jam.
Petits Fours: Pipe 1 cm/½in rounds. When baked sandwich together with apricot jam and half dip into melted chocolate.

Serving suggestion: Serve as afternoon tea. Also ideal for wedding functions.

Freezing: Will freeze for up to 3 months, or keep for 2 weeks in an airtight container.

Norfolk Rings

Makes 16   Preparation time: 35 minutes   Baking time: 20 minutes

Confectioners' custard is used extensively in baking and adds a delicate flavour to Danish Pastry. It keeps the Danish moist when baked and can be served as a sauce.

For the pastry:
900g/2lb Danish Pastry
  (page 110)

For the custard filling:
275ml/½ pint milk, boiled
25g/1oz sugar
2 teaspoons cornflour
2 eggs
Vanilla essence to taste
175g/6oz apples, chopped
75g/3oz sultanas
1 teaspoon nutmeg

For the egg wash:
1 egg beaten with milk

For the glaze:
100g/4oz apricot jam, boiled
100g/4oz water icing
50g/2oz flaked almonds, roasted

Use 2 × 30cm/12in baking sheets, well oiled

Pre-heat the oven to 200°C/400°F/Gas Mark 6
Microwave: After 5 minutes transfer to a conventional oven to brown. For best results bake in the conventional oven only.

---

1   Make the custard filling by boiling the milk. Mix the sugar, cornflour and eggs to form a paste. Add to the milk and stir till thickened. Add the vanilla essence. Allow to cool before using.

---

2   Roll out the pastry to 5mm/¼in thickness and form into a rectangle. Egg wash the surface and spread the custard thinly over ¾ of the surface. Sprinkle the apples, sultanas and spice on top of the custard. Fold the plain side over the filling and again the other side to form 3 layers. Roll out to 25cm/10in wide.

3   Cut into 1cm/½in strips. Twist each one and join the ends to form a ring. Place on a baking sheet well spaced. Egg wash and prove for 30 minutes. Bake till golden brown.

4   Glaze with hot apricot jam. Allow to cool. Repeat with water icing and finish with a sprinkling of nuts.

Variations: To make finger shapes, just leave in strips and bake as above. Almond filling can be used instead of custard.

Serving suggestion: Serve as a snack with mugs of hot chocolate on Guy Fawkes night.

Freezing: Will freeze unbaked for 3 months or baked for 2 months.

Golden Treacle Tart

Makes 2 tarts   Preparation time: 20 minutes   Baking time: 20—30 minutes

The north of England is renowned for its variety of tongue-clicking tarts and pies. A simple one to make is the treacle tart. Use any breadcrumbs left over from breadmaking.

For the tarts:
450g/1lb Sweet Pastry (page 85)

For the filling:
350ml/12floz Golden Syrup
100g/4oz breadcrumbs
25g/1oz sesame seeds
Zest and juice of a lemon
Pinch of ginger

Use 2 × 20cm/8in round tart plates

Pre-heat the oven to approximately 190°C/375°F/Gas Mark 5
Microwave: From 3—12 minutes and then transfer to conventional oven to brown.

1   Roll out the pastry and line 2 tart plates. Trim the edges.

2   Divide the syrup and pour into each case. Sprinkle with breadcrumbs mixed with sesame seeds. Add the juice and zest and ginger on top of the syrup.

3   Bake in the oven for 20—30 minutes until golden in colour.

Variations: Add currants, chopped walnuts or coconut instead of the seeds. Save some pastry and cut some strips. Interweave the pastry on top of the filling to form a pattern.

Serving suggestion: Serve hot or cold with brandy-flavoured whipped cream. Try a slice with lemon sorbet made with yoghurt. Truly a tart with a heart!

Freezing: Up to 3 months.

Mac-a-Mince Tart

Makes 2   Preparation time: 20 minutes   Baking time: 20—30 minutes

In this recipe I have combined the fruitiness of mincemeat and the nuttiness of almonds to make an anytime treat. The piped topping can vary in design to suit the occasion.

For the tarts:
450g/1lb Sweet Pastry (page 85)

For the filling:
225g/8oz mincemeat

For the topping:
100g/4oz almonds, ground
100g/4oz caster sugar
100g/4oz granulated sugar
15g/½oz ground rice
1 egg white

Use 2 × 20cm/8in round tart plates

Pre-heat the oven to 190°C/375°F/Gas Mark 5
Microwave: From 3—5 minutes and then transfer to the conventional oven to brown.

1   Roll out the pastry and line the tart plates. Trim the edges.

2   Divide the mincemeat and spread onto each tart case.

3   For the topping, mix the almonds, sugar and rice together. Place the egg white in a bowl and add the dry ingredients. Beat for 3 minutes in the food processor on a medium speed. Using a 1cm/½in plain piping tube to make lattice lines of the almond mixture on top.

4   Bake for 20—30 minutes until golden in colour.

Variations: Pipe in various designs to change the appearance, e.g. spiral, zig-zag, criss-cross or just plain. Instead of mincemeat use apples, apricots, blackcurrants and so on.

Serving suggestion: Serve hot or cold with rum-flavoured egg custard or whipped cream. A slice of tart with grapefruit sorbet goes down a treat.

Freezing: Will freeze for up to 3 months, or keep for 12 days in an airtight tin.

Linton Linz Slice

Makes 2   Preparation time: 25 minutes   Baking time: 20—30 minutes

A rich hazelnut pastry with layers of almond filling topped with appetising apricots.

For the slice:
100g/4oz butter
100g/4oz sugar
1 egg
50g/2oz hazelnuts, ground
250g/9oz soft flour
Pinch of salt
Pinch of cinnamon

For the topping:
100g/4oz butter
100g/4oz caster sugar
2 eggs
75g/3oz almonds, ground
25g/1oz cake crumbs
Almond or vanilla essence
1 medium tin apricots
50g/2oz glacé cherries

For the glaze:
50g/2oz apricot jam

Use 30cm/12in baking sheet, well oiled

Pre-heat the oven to 190°C/375°F/Gas Mark 5
Microwave: After 8 minutes transfer to a conventional oven to brown.

---

1   Cream together the butter and sugar. Add the egg and blend in the hazelnuts, flour, salt and cinnamon. Form a paste but don't overmix. Roll out the pastry to a length of 30cm/12in. Cut into 10cm/4in strips. Line the baking sheet with these. Pinch edges to form a border or cut 5mm/¼in long strips, place on dampened edges and pinch together. Spread a little jam down the centre.

---

2   For the topping, cream together the butter and sugar till light. Add the eggs and blend in the almonds and cake crumbs. Mix in the essence and mix to a batter. Using a 1cm/½in plain piping tube, pipe the almond mixture onto the pastry strips, or use a spoon. Position the apricots in pairs across the length of the pastry. Finish with the glacé cherries dotted in between the apricots.

3   With the leftover pastry make a smooth paste with a little water. Pipe a zig-zag pattern along the top. Bake in a moderate oven for 20—30 minutes until golden in colour. Glaze with apricot jam.

Variations: Use any fruits available or just dried fruit mixed in with the filling and a sprinkling of toasted flaked hazelnuts. Make individual fruit tarts if you prefer.

Serving suggestion: Serve as a dessert with a light ginger custard which makes a refreshing change from heavy puddings. Or serve on its own for afternoon tea.

Freezing: Will freeze for up to 3 months, or keep for 1 week in the fridge.

Peter's Pumpkin Pie with Cranberries

Makes 2   Preparation time: 35 minutes   Baking time: 20—30 minutes

An American favourite at Hallowe'en. Use the pumpkin for the pie filling and make a mask from the skin.

For the pie pastry
150g/5oz butter
50g/2oz sugar
1 egg
225g/8oz soft flour
Pinch of salt
Pinch of cinnamon

For the filling:
275ml/½ pint pumpkin purée
25g/1oz flour
Pinch of salt
50g/2oz sugar
½ teaspoon ginger
½ teaspoon cinnamon
½ teaspoon nutmeg
2 eggs
50g/2oz whipped cream
1 tablespoon rum
*Zest and juice of a lemon or
  orange*
50g/2oz cranberries

Use 2 × 20cm/8in round pie dishes, well oiled

Pre-heat the oven to 200°C/400°F/Gas Mark 6
Microwave: After 8 minutes, transfer to a conventional oven to brown.

1 Cream the butter and sugar. Add the egg and blend in the flour, salt and cinnamon. Form a paste but don't overmix. Roll out the pastry and line 2 pie tins. Pinch the edges to form a border.

2   For the filling, boil the pumpkin, sieve cool and add the flour, salt, sugar and spices. Separate the eggs, beat the yolks and mix into the pumpkin. Blend in the whipped cream, rum, zest and juice. Finally fold in the egg white and clear.

3   Spread the mixture into the pastry cases and smooth over. Place the cranberries to form the outline of a face. Bake for 20—30 minutes until golden in colour.

Variations: Use any fruits available or just add dried fruit to the filling. Make individual pies and for the faces cut out any leftover bits of pastry.

Serving suggestion: Serve as a highlight at a Hallowe'en party with plenty of liquid refreshment! Don't be afraid to eat more than 2 slices.

Freezing: Will freeze for up to 1 month, or keep for 1 week in the fridge.

Rough and Puff Pastry

Makes 1175g/2lb 8oz   Preparation time: 45 minutes
Baking time: 20—30 minutes

Although the layers of flaky pastry rise to any occasion, care is always needed in its creation. Puff pastry goes well with any fruit, nut or savoury filling.

For the pastry:
450g/1lb strong white flour
75g/3oz butter
Pinch of salt
275ml/½ pint cold water
1 teaspoon lemon juice
400g/14oz butter or lard

Pre-heat the oven to 200°C/400°F/Gas Mark 6
Microwave: After 6 minutes transfer to a conventional oven to brown.

---

1   Place the flour, butter and salt into a mixing bowl and blend together. Add the cold water and the lemon juice and mix to form an elastic dough. Rest for 10 minutes.

---

2   Roll out the pastry dough into a rectangle. Cut the butter into slices and cover three-quarters of the pastry. Fold over the other quarter to cover the butter. Complete by folding again. There should be three layers of pastry enclosing the butter. Repeat this process 6 times, resting the pastry after every 2 turns for 10 minutes in the fridge. Rest before cutting out.

---

3   The pastry is now ready for cutting out into various shapes. The time it takes to make is well worth the trouble. Use for pies, turnover, slices, horns, palmiers, savouries, vol-au-vents, etc.

---

4   Bake in a moderate oven as above until golden in colour for approximately 20—30 minutes.

Variations: Rough Puff: Chop the butter or lard into cubes. Add to the dry ingredients. Mix in the water to form a dough, making sure the butter remains in cubes when mixed. Give only 3 turns. The pastry is now ready. Puff pastry has no sugar so it is ideal for sweet confections as well as savoury.

Freezing: Will freeze unbaked for 6 months or keep for 1 week in the fridge.

Left Country Manor Bread (page 14). **Right** Wholemeal Baps and Batons (page 22).

Top Easter Buns *(page 44)*. **Centre** *Portland Nut Roulade (page 62)*.
Bottom *Chocolate Almond Plait (page 60)*.

Top left Dartmoor Demons (page 82). **Top right** *Bran and Raisin Muffins (page 79).*
Centre *Countryman Scones (page 74).* **Centre right** *Oaties (page 75).*
Bottom left *Elizabethan Fritters (page 80).*

Top *Caramel Butterflies (page 103).* **Centre left** *Linton Linz Slice (page 92).*
Centre right *Congress Tarts (page 87).* **Bottom** *Choux Pastry Eclairs (page 106).*

Maids of Honour

Make 12 tarts   Preparation time: 35 minutes   Baking time: 30 minutes

The genuine Maid of Honour has a curd cheese filling which was originally made from rennet-curdled milk mixed with butter, eggs, almonds, sugar and spice. This recipe dates back a very long way.

For the pastry:
450g Rough and Puff Pastry
  (page 96)
50g/2oz lemon curd

For the filling:
575ml/1 pint warm milk
  (38°C/100°F)
1 teaspoon rennet
225g/8oz butter

225g/8oz sugar
2 eggs
50g/2oz almonds, ground
1 teaspoon nutmeg
Zest and juice of a lemon
2 teaspoons brandy

For the topping:
50g/2oz almonds, flaked

Use 12 × 7.5cm/3in shallow patty tins, well oiled

Pre-heat the oven to 200°C/400°F/Gas Mark 6
Microwave: After 3 minutes transfer to a conventional oven to brown.

1 To make the filling, place the warm milk in a bowl with the rennet and leave for 2—3 hours. Squeeze out the moisture and sieve the curds. Cream the butter and sugar together and add the eggs. Beat to a light consistency. Blend in the almonds, spice, lemon juice and zest, and the brandy. Finally add the curds and mix to clear.

2 Roll out the pastry. Cut it to line the 12 patty tins. Pipe a spot of lemon curd in each one. Pipe or spoon the filling into each pastry case. Sprinkle almonds on the top. Rest for 20 minutes before baking or shrinkage may occur.

3 Bake until golden brown for 15—30 minutes.

Variations: Any jam can be used in the base. The introduction of dried fruits can make the maids more interesting.

Serving suggestion: Serve at teatime with carefully made cups of Earl Grey tea.

Freezing: Will freeze unbaked for 3 months or keep for 1 week in a container.

Thousand Layer Cream Slice

Makes 1   Preparation time: 35 minutes   Baking time: 15—20 minutes

Everybody's favourite temptation. To avoid the filling oozing out between the layers of flaky pastry I have adjusted the recipe so the creamy centre stays intact.

For the pastry layers:
450g/1lb Rough and Puff Pastry
  or cuttings (page 96)

For the filling:
225ml/8fl oz milk
2 egg yolks
50g/2oz sugar
Pinch of salt
225g/8oz cream cheese
50g/2oz sultanas
Zest and juice of a lemon
275g/10oz whipped cream
25g/1oz gelatin
125ml/ 4fl oz warm water

For the topping:
100g/4oz Fondant Icing
  (page 178)

Use 1 × 30cm/12in baking sheet, well oiled

Pre-heat the oven to 200°C/400°F/Gas Mark 6
Microwave: After 3 minutes transfer to a conventional oven to brown.

---

1   Roll out the pastry to 5mm/¼in thickness. Cut into 30cm/12in long by 10cm/4in wide strips. With a fork prick all over the surface to stop any air pockets from forming during baking. Rest for 10 minutes before baking blind for 15—20 minutes.

---

2   When baked, melt the fondant over a bain marie and coat the smooth side of the pastry.

3   To make the filling, boil the milk. Mix the egg yolks, sugar and salt together. Add the milk whilst continuing to boil this over the heat until thickened, stirring all the time. When cold take a little of this 'custard' and mix with the cheese. Continue adding until smooth and clear. Add the fruits, including zest and juice, and carefully blend in the whipped cream.

4   Dissolve the gelatin in the warm water and slowly pour into the rest of the filling to produce a light creamy texture.

5   While still soft, sandwich 2 layers of pastry with the filling in between. Make sure the fondant side of the pastry is on top. Smooth the edges with a palette knife. Place in the fridge to set before cutting.

Variations: To save time just use whipped cream for a filling with a thin layer of raspberry jam. Cut the strips of pastry into portions before placing onto the filling as it makes it easier to cut through the slice.

Serving suggestion: Serve as a dessert with a glass of sweet white wine. A thousand good reasons to enjoy another slice!

Freezing: Will freeze unbaked for 3 months or keep for 1 week in the fridge.

Autumn Strudel

Makes 1   Preparation time: 25 minutes   Baking time: 20—35 minutes

The fruits of autumn are gathered together to make this Continental variation. Any available soft fresh fruit will do. Apples are used as the base.

For the pastry:
450g/1lb Rough and Puff Pastry
  or cuttings (page 96)

For the filling:
100g/4oz butter, melted
150g/5oz breadcrumbs, toasted
100g/4oz sugar
1 teaspoon cinnamon

225g/8oz apples, cooked
225g/8oz blackberries, cooked
100g/4oz blackcurrants, cooked
100g/4oz redcurrants, cooked
75g/3oz raisins
1 tablespoon Madeira wine

For the topping:
50g/2oz icing sugar

Use a 30cm/12in baking sheet, well oiled

Pre-heat the oven to 200°C/400°F/Gas Mark 6
Microwave: After 5 minutes transfer to a conventional oven to brown.

1   Roll out the pastry to 5mm/¼in thickness. Form a square of 30cm/12in size. Spread the melted butter over the surface and sprinkle on the breadcrumbs, sugar and cinnamon. Mix all the fruits together with the wine and cover the pastry with this mixture, leaving a 5cm/2in border.

2   Fold the edges over to cover the fruit. Seal the ends and place on a baking sheet, the joins at the bottom. Brush with butter and rest for 10 minutes.

3   Bake in moderate oven for approximately 30 minutes till crisp and golden.

Variations: If the fruit is very juicy, add extra breadcrumbs and use any fruit left over as a garnish when serving. Mincemeat makes a good alternative at Christmas time. Add rum instead of the wine for a richer flavour.

Serving suggestion: Serve cut into slices with whirls of fresh, whipped cream and a sauce of puréed, mixed fresh berries.

Freezing: Will freeze unbaked for 3 months or keep for 1 week in the fridge.

Conversation Tarts

Makes 12   Preparation time: 35 minutes   Baking time: 15—30 minutes

The ladies who gathered at the Olde Tea Rooms, near Little Buxford in Oxfordshire, were always nattering on about this and that. One thing they all agreed on was that every afternoon they should partake in enjoying their Conversation Tarts, unless of course, they ran out!

For the pastry:
675g/1lb 8oz Rough and Puff
* Pastry (page 96)*
50g/2oz strawberry jam

For the topping:
2 tablespoons icing sugar
1 teaspoon cornflour
Few drops of water

For the filling:
350g/12oz Bakewell filling
* (page 111)*

Use 12 × 7.5cm/3in shallow patty tins, well oiled

Pre-heat the oven to 200°C/400°F/Gas Mark 6
Microwave: After 3 minutes transfer to a conventional oven to brown.

---

1   Thinly roll out the pastry. Cut it and line 12 patty tins. Pipe a spot of jam into the centre of each tart. Pipe or spoon in the Bakewell filling to each tart. For the tops cut 12 lids, moisten edges and cover the filling. Seal and pierce to allow the air to escape. Rest for 20 minutes before baking or shrinkage may occur.

---

2   For the topping, mix the icing sugar and cornflour together and add a few drops of water to form a smooth paste. Spread this thinly over the top of each tart so that they are completely covered. Cut 4 strips of pastry, each 7.5cm/3in long and place on top in diamond shapes.

---

3   Bake for between 15—30 minutes until golden in colour.

Variations: Use any leftover Royal icing for the tops. Just add a little cornflour to form a crusty finish. A choice of cheese or fruit can be used instead of the Bakewell.

Serving suggestion: Serve at teaparties. Guaranteed to heighten any conversation!

Freezing: Will freeze unbaked for 3 months or keep for 1 week in a container.

Summer Fruit Pizza

Makes 2   Preparation time: 25 minutes   Baking time: 20—35 minutes

Summer is the time for barbecues and picnics. What better way to finish a main course than with a colourful design of fresh fruits on a bed of flaky pastry.

For the pastry base:
450g/1lb Rough and Puff Pastry
  (page 96)
100g/4oz Choux Pastry
  (page 104)

100g/4oz strawberries
1 peach, peeled and sliced
1 kiwifruit, peeled and sliced
100g/4oz apricot jam, boiled

For the filling:
225g/8oz Cheese filling
  (page 123)
100g/4oz raspberries

For the topping:
50g/2oz flaked almonds

Use 2 × 30cm/12in baking sheets, well oiled

Pre-heat the oven to 200°C/400°F/Gas Mark 6
Microwave: After 5 minutes transfer to a conventional oven to brown.

---

1   Roll out the pastry to 5mm/¼in thickness. Cut 2 circles of 20cm/8in diameter. Prick with a fork. Pipe a ring of choux pastry around the edges. Place each circle onto greased baking sheets and rest for 15 minutes before baking blind.

---

2   When baked and cool spread the cheese filling into each case. Using different coloured fruits, arrange them alternately starting in the centre and moving outwards. Cover the circles completely. Glaze the fruit with the boiled apricot jam and finish with flaked almonds.

Variations: Use any fruit available. Try a base of custard instead of the cheese filling.

Serving suggestion: Serve hot or cold with a lemon sauce or a scoop of orange sorbet. Alternatively, cut into slices with whirls of fresh whipped cream and a sauce of puréed raspberries.

Freezing: Will freeze for 3 months or keep for 1 week in the fridge.

Caramel Butterflies

Makes 12   Preparation time: 25 minutes   Baking time: 15—20 minutes

Having been asked to make caramel butterflies for my children, I set about the task with relish. The golden crisp bite of hot sugar interspersed with layers of flaky pastry is more than one can resist! Finding a plateful had vanished before my eyes, my son retorted 'They must have flown away!'.

For the pastry:
450g/1lb Rough and Puff Pastry
(page 96)

50ml/2fl oz water
100g/4oz caster sugar

Use 2 × 30cm/12in baking sheets, well oiled

Pre-heat the oven to 200°C/400°F/Gas Mark 6
Microwave: After 3 minutes transfer to a conventional oven to brown.

---

1   Thinly roll out the pastry to a square or rectangle. Mark the centre with a knife. Dampen and sprinkle caster sugar over the surface. Fold from both ends towards the centre line leaving a small gap. Dampen again and sprinkle once more with caster sugar. Fold towards the centre again. Finally repeat once more to form a long strip. With a thin rolling pin indent the middle.

---

2   Cut pieces 5mm/¼in thick and place on the baking sheets, with the folded edges facing down. Allow plenty of room for expansion. Rest for 20 minutes before baking.

---

3   Bake for 15—20 minutes until golden in colour. Turn over to complete baking.

Variations: Palmiers are made in the same way, except do not indent before cutting. Finish off by sandwiching 2 together with jam and whipped cream. Horns are made by cutting the rolled-out pastry into 40cm/16in × 2.5/1in strips. Use a metal horn or pepperpot. Starting from the wide end, roll the strips around the horn to the pointed end making sure that the pastry overlaps. Horns should be greased prior to starting in order that the pastry does not stick. Dip the tops in sugar and bake as above.

Serving suggestion: Serve instead of biscuits, but store only under lock and key as they have a tendency to disappear into thin air!

Freezing: Will freeze unbaked for 3 months or keep for several weeks in a container.

Basic Choux Pastry

Makes 450g/1lb pastry   Preparation time: 25 minutes

This basic choux pastry can be used for many of the recipes in this book. It is perhaps best to make at least 450g/1lb and store any which you do not immediately require in the freezer.

275ml/½ pint water
175g/6oz margarine
200g/7oz strong white flour
275ml/½ pint eggs, mixed

---

1   In a large saucepan bring the water to the boil with the margarine. Then add the flour and stir till a roux forms. On a low heat cook for a further 5 minutes, making sure that the mixture does not stick to the sides of the pan.

---

2   Transfer the roux to a mixing bowl. Gradually add the eggs and beat well for 5 minutes until the mixture is clear and light in appearance. The pastry is ready to be used for any recipe, it can be piped through piping tubes or worked with a spoon.

Freezing: The choux pastry will keep in an airtight container in the refrigerator for up to 1 week.

St George's Slice

Makes 1   Preparation time: 25 minutes   Baking time: 30 minutes

Coffee and mandarins go well together in this recipe. I have soaked a sponge cake in Cointreau and magically produced a sumptuous dream dessert.

The Choux Pastry (page 104)

For the filling:
1 x 15cm/6in plain sponge cake
2 tablespoons Cointreau
225ml/8oz whipped cream
1 tin mandarins

For the topping:
100g/4oz apricot jam, boiled
100g/4oz Fondant Icing (page 178)
1 teaspoon instant coffee
50g/2oz walnuts, chopped

Use 2 × 30cm/12in baking sheets, well oiled

Pre-heat the oven to 200°C/400°F/Gas Mark 6
Microwave: After 5 minutes transfer to a conventional oven to brown. For best results bake in conventional oven completely.

---

1   Using a 2.5cm/1in piping tube, pipe 2 long lines of choux pastry 30cm/12in on a baking sheet so that they join together. Allow room between strips to expand. Bake at above heat for 20—30 minutes till light and dry. When baked, cut and divide in half. For the top take one half and glaze with jam. Melt the fondant and add the coffee to it. Cover the top half with it and dip into chopped walnuts.

---

2   Cut and shape the sponge cake to fit the slice. Soak in Cointreau. Place on the base of the slice and pipe whipped cream over the sponge. Add the mardarins. Place the top section on the whipped cream and cut into portions.

Variations: Fruit cake soaked makes a different filling and will appeal to lovers of Christmas pudding. Instead of apricot purée and fondant, dip the choux slice in boiled sugar which has reached a temperature of 174°C/345°F.

Serving suggestion: Serve on Christmas Day instead of the pudding. Use brandy instead of Cointreau to add a festive flair.

Freezing: Will freeze un-glazed for 3 months or keep for 3 days in the fridge.

Choux Pastry Eclairs

Makes 30   Preparation time: 35 minutes   Baking time: 30—35 minutes

A soft pastry requiring a piping bag or spoon to deposit. It is not easy to make but the results produce light, crispy soft cushions, filled with cream and topped with soft chocolate icing. Irresistible!

The Choux Pastry (page 104)

For the filling:
225ml/8fl oz whipped cream

For the topping:
100g/4oz chocolate, melted
225g/8oz fondant

Use 2 × 30cm/12in baking sheets, well oiled

Pre-heat the oven to 220°C/425°F/Gas Mark 7
Microwave: After 5 minutes transfer to a conventional oven.

1   In a large saucepan bring to the boil the water and margarine. Add the flour and stir till a roux forms. On a low heat cook for a further 5 minutes. The roux should not stick to the sides.

2   Transfer the roux to a mixing bowl. Gradually add the eggs and beat for 5 minutes until clear and light. Using a 1cm/½in piping tube, pipe 10cm/4in eclairs onto the baking sheets allowing room to expand. Bake in a moderate oven as above for 30 minutes until light and airy.

3   When baked and cool cut down the centre of each eclair. Melt the fondant and chocolate together in a bain marie. Dip the tops of the eclairs in the mixture and allow to set. Fill each one with whipped cream. Place in paper cases and serve.

Variations: Choux buns are made the same way but piped round instead of lengthwise. Replace cream with custard or cream cheese filling. The icing can vary in flavour by adding coffee, strawberry, lemon or any other flavour you like.

Serving suggestion: Serve as a sweet or afternoon pastry with a cup of espresso coffee.

Freezing: Will freeze un-iced for up to 3 months or keep in the fridge for 3 days.

Sundae Tea Choux

Makes 30   Preparation time: 25 minutes   Baking time: 30—35 minutes

Choux buns are a good medium for all sorts of desserts. To achieve large buns they should be baked in coffins — that is, covered with a bread tin to keep the steam in and produce a light textured bun suitable for filling.

The Choux Pastry (page 104)

For the filling:
225ml/8floz whipped cream

For the topping:
2 tablespoons kirsch

100g/4oz strawberries
225g/8oz mixed, freshly cut fruits
  (grapes, oranges, bananas,
  pineapple)
100g/4oz apricot jam, boiled

Use 2 × 30cm/12in baking sheets, well oiled

Pre-heat the oven to 220°C/425°F/Gas Mark 7
Microwave: After 5 minutes transfer to a conventional oven to brown. For best results bake in a conventional oven.

1   In a large saucepan bring the water and margarine to the boil. Add the flour and stir till a roux forms. On a low heat cook for a further 5 minutes. The roux should not stick to the sides.

2   Transfer the roux to a mixing bowl and gradually add the eggs. Beat for 5 minutes till clear and light. Using a 1cm/½in piping tube, pipe 3cm/1½in round buns onto a baking sheet allowing room for expansion. If you wish to increase the volume, cover with bread tins. Bake for 30—35 minutes.

3   When baked and cool, cut in half. Fill the bottom half with whipped cream. Soak the fruits in the kirsch for 1 hour. Turn the other half over and arrange a selection of the fruits on top of each shell finishing with a strawberry in the centre. Glaze with boiled apricot purée. Cool. Place the completed half on the cream base. Store in the fridge till required.

Variations: Pipe choux mixture into the shape of a banana. When baked, cut in half and fill the base with cream. Cut a banana lengthwise and place on the top of the cream. Replace the 'lid'. Glaze with purée and sprinkle with flaked chocolate or almonds for what's called a Bananarama.

Serving suggestion: Serve as a sweet with a strawberry sauce. The Bananarama can be served with a hot rum-flavoured chocolate sauce.

Freezing: Will freeze unfinished for 3 months or keep for 3 days in the fridge.

Petits Choux Pyramids

Makes 65 choux   Preparation time: 25 minutes   Baking time: 15—20 minutes

In France the centrepiece at any formal occasion would nearly always include a Croquembouche — a monument to any great pastrycook. Let's try a smaller version.

The Choux Pastry (page 104)

For the filling:
225ml/8fl oz whipped cream

For the base:
1 ×175g/6oz sponge cake,
  shaped into a dome
2 tablespoons rum
100g/4oz strawberry jam
100g/4oz whipped cream

For the topping:
225g/8oz apricot jam, boiled
2 tablespoons rum

Use 2 × 30cm/12in baking sheets, well oiled

Pre-heat the oven to 200°C/400°F/Gas Mark 6
Microwave: After 5 minutes transfer to a conventional oven to brown. For best results bake completely in the conventional oven.

---

1   Using a 1cm/½in piping tube, pipe 1cm/½in round buns of the pastry onto the baking sheets, allowing room to expand. Bake in a moderate oven for 15—20 minutes till light and dry.

---

2   Cut and shape the sponge to resemble a pyramid. Soak with rum, layer and fill with jam and whipped cream. Place on a dish.

---

3   Dip or glaze each choux bun in the boiled apricot and rum mixture. Arrange around the outside of the sponge, building up to a pyramid or dome. (Maximum height 30cm/12in.) Decorate the top with crystallised flowers. Finish with a light sprinkling of nibbed almonds. Store in a cool place and serve the same day as making.

Variations: Instead of apricot purée dip the choux buns in boiled sugar which has reached a temperature of 174°C/345°F. This will produce a toffee-substance and will stick the choux buns better than the jam. To spin the sugar, dip a fork in the boiled sugar and between 2 poles or sticks spin the sugar moving back and forwards. The strands will form over the poles. Collect the spun sugar and ball up. Place on top of the pyramid to imitate a waterfall.

Serving suggestion: Serve on special occasions as a special feature. The effect will bring admiring glances every time.

Freezing: Will freeze unglazed for 3 months or keep for 3 days in the fridge.

Danish Pastry

Makes 1kg/2lb   Preparation time: 35 minutes   Baking time: 20 minutes

Danish pastry is an enriched puff pastry. Yeast is used to produce a mellow eating quality which, combined with nuts and fruits, makes it an appetising confection.

For the pastry:
450g/1lb strong white flour
25g/1oz milk powder
Pinch of salt
25g/1oz sugar

25g/1oz butter
1 large egg
20g/¾oz yeast
175ml/6fl oz cold water
275g/10oz butter or lard

Use 2 × 30cm/12in baking sheets, well oiled
Pre-heat the oven to 200°C/400°F/Gas Mark 6
Microwave: After 5 minutes transfer to a conventional oven to brown. For best results bake completely in the conventional oven.

1   Blend together the flour, milk powder, salt and sugar. Mix in the butter and the egg. Dissolve the yeast in the water and add to the mixture. Mix to a smooth elastic dough. Rest for 30 minutes in an oiled polythene bag.

2   Roll out the pastry to a rectangular shape. Cover with ¾ of the butter or lard. Fold over to cover the butter and then complete by turning the whole thing over. Repeat this procedure twice more using the remaining butter or lard. Rest for 15 minutes in the fridge before shaping.

Secret tip: For best results make sure the dough and butter are the same consistency, otherwise the butter may bake out of the pastry, which would be a waste. When proving, avoid too hot an area as the butter may melt. For speed use the Rough and Puff method (page 96) for mixing the dough.

Serving suggestion: Serve as a covering for all types of fillings or just on its own.

Freezing: Will freeze unbaked for 3 months or keep for 2 days in the fridge.

Bakewell Tarts

Makes 2   Preparation time: 25 minutes   Baking time: 20–25 minutes

Originally called Bakewell Pudding, an accident by a cook omitting the flour in a rich almond cake resulted in the creation of Bakewell Tarts.

For the tarts:
450g/1lb Sweet Pastry (page 85)
100g/4oz strawberry jam

75g/3oz ground almonds
25g/1oz cake crumbs
Almond or vanilla essence

For the filling:
100g/4oz butter
100g/4oz caster sugar
2 eggs

For the glaze:
50g/2oz apricot jam
50g/2oz water icing (see Note)

Use 2 × 20cm/8in round, 2.5cm/1in deep sandwich tins

Pre-heat the oven to 190°C/375°F/Gas Mark 5
Microwave: After 10 minutes transfer to a conventional oven to brown.

---

1 Roll out the pastry and line the sandwich tins. Trim the edges and spread a little jam in the centre of each.

---

2 To make the filling, cream the butter and the sugar until they form a light mixture. Add the egg and blend in the almonds and the crumbs. Mix in the essence and mix well to form a batter. Using a 1cm/½in plain piping tube, half fill the sandwich tins with the mixture or spread with a spoon.

---

3 Roll out the leftover pastry until very thin. Cut circles from this and place in a design on top of the tarts.

---

4 Bake until golden in colour. Glaze with apricot jam and icing.

Variations: For decoration place a glacé cherry in the centre or sprinkle with flaked, roasted nuts. Instead of jam, try apples, currants or raisins soaked in sherry.

Serving suggestion: Serve as a pudding with raspberry sauce, or on its own.

Freezing: Will freeze for up to 3 months, or keep for 1 week in an airtight container.

Note: Water icing is a very simple mix of water and icing sugar, mixed to your own desired strength. A little lemon juice might be added.

Tangy Slice

Makes 2   Preparation time: 25 minutes   Baking time: 30 minutes

Dates have been used for centuries as a sweetmeat. In cooking they impart a richness to cakes, pastries, sweets and desserts. One can almost hear the rustle of palms!

For the pastry:
450g/1lb Danish Pastry
  (page 110)

For the filling:
225g/8oz dates, minced
175g/6oz apples, chopped
175g/6oz sugar
225g/8oz cake crumbs
75ml/3fl oz orange juice
Zest of an orange
1 egg
½ teaspoon mixed spice
Egg wash

For the glaze:
100g/4oz apricot jam, boiled
100g/4oz water icing
50g/2oz sesame seeds

Use 2 × 30cm/12in baking sheets, well oiled

Pre-heat the oven to 200°C/400°F/Gas Mark 6
Microwave: After 5 minutes transfer to a conventional oven to brown. For best results use a conventional oven only.

---

1 For the filling, mince the dates and the apples. Add the sugar, cake crumbs, orange juice and zest. Mix to a paste. Finally add the egg and spice and mix till clear.

---

2 Roll out the pastry to 5mm/¼in thickness and form a rectangle. Cut 10cm/4in wide strips, allowing 2 per slice. Place the base strips on the baking sheets and egg wash the surface of each one. Spread the filling along the middle leaving 1cm/½in borders. Cover the slice with the other strip and seal the edges. Make slanted cuts on the top so that the filling shows. Egg wash and prove for 30 minutes.

112

3   Bake for 30 minutes until golden brown. Glaze with hot apricot jam and allow
    to cool. Repeat with the water icing and finish with a sprinkling of seeds.

Variations: *Dartmoor Slice:* Replace the date filling with a custard base topped with cherry pie filling.
Tropical Surprise: Chop a mango, banana and a little pineapple instead of the
dates and apples. Finish with a sprinkling of coconut.

Serving suggestion: Serve on picnics with glasses of homemade ginger ale.

Freezing: Will freeze unbaked for 3 months or baked for 2 months.

Almond Whirls

Makes 1kg/2lb pastry   Preparation time: 35 minutes   Baking time: 20 minutes

The many varieties of things one can make using Danish Pastry could fill a book on their own. Here are just a few to get you started. Try to experiment and the results will surprise you.

For the pastry:
900g/2lb Danish Pastry
(page 110)

For the egg wash:
1 egg beaten with milk

For the filling:
225g/8oz marzipan
1 egg white
100g/4oz currants
1 teaspoon cinnamon

For the glaze:
100g/4oz apricot jam, boiled
100g/4oz Fondant Icing
  (page 178)
75g/3oz glacé cherries
50g/2oz flaked almonds, roasted

Use 2 × 30cm/12in baking sheets, well oiled

Pre-heat the oven to 200°C/400°F/Gas Mark 6
Microwave: After 5 minutes transfer to a conventional oven to brown. For best results use the conventional oven only.

---

1   Roll out the pastry to 5mm/¼in thickness. Egg wash the surface. Spread a mixture of marzipan and egg white over the pastry but leave the edges free. Sprinkle currants and cinnamon over the filling. Roll up Swiss-roll fashion to form a long sausage. Egg wash the surface.

---

2   Cut into 1cm/½in slices. Place cut-side-down on the baking sheets, well spaced to allow for expansion. Prove for 30 minutes in a warm place.

---

3   Bake for 20 minutes and then glaze with hot apricot jam and allow to cool. Top with icing and finish with half a cherry and a sprinkling of nuts.

Variations: *Croissants:* Roll out the pastry as above and cut into 12.5cm/5in wide strips. Cut triangles from each strip and egg wash. Roll up from the widest end to the tip and place on oiled baking sheets. Egg wash the tops, prove and bake as normal. Eat hot with butter.

Turnovers: Follow the same procedure as for Croissants except that instead of triangles, cut squares. Egg wash and place a suitable filling (fruits, etc) in the centre. Fold over from one corner to the opposite one to form triangular shapes. Egg wash, prove and bake. Other shapes to try include sausage rolls and cushions (made like turnovers but each corner is folded to the centre). Fillings can include praline, chocolate, custard and cheese as well as various dried fruits.

Serving suggestion: Serve as a snack or as teatime pastries.

Freezing: Will freeze unbaked for 3 months or baked 2 months.

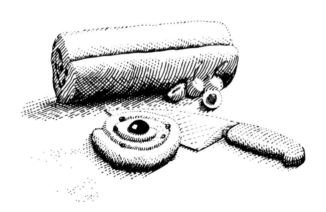

CHAPTER 5

PROVINCIAL SNACKS, SAVOURIES AND PIES

Medieval times set the scene for many of our ancestral traditions. The ubiquitous meat pie was praised for the manner in which all kinds of unusual fillings were stuffed into delicately short (in the sense of light and crumbly) eating casings. Admired savouries were the creation of cooks who prided themselves on using the finest produce available — wild boar, venison, swan and many varieties of game.

For centuries the kitchen was the centre of many a grand feast, and later once-a-week bake-ins kept the tradition alive. Farm produce joined forces with new produce from abroad — spices, sugars, dates, fruits and other exotic imports — resulting in exciting new combinations and recipes.

Savouries, as distinct from sweeter delicacies, were served at the beginning and the end of the meal. In Victorian days the savoury was eaten as a small tit-bit before the last course, and it was introduced to aid the digestion which was needed as eating was very much an event.

Today the savoury is still popular but now as a main course, snack or anytime nibble. No longer do we spend days feasting at the table but the recipes in this chapter offer a chance to recapture some of the old-style dishes that were so popular.

Mac-a-Vegi Flan

Makes 1   Preparation time: 45 minutes   Baking time: 30 minutes

For the pastry:
225g/8oz Basic Savoury Pastry
  (page 118)

For the filling:
100g/4oz macaroni, cooked al
  dente
1 small onion
1 clove garlic
½ green pepper, sliced
50g/2oz celery, sliced
50g/2oz mushroom, sliced
50g/2oz sweetcorn

20g/¾oz butter
20g/¾oz flour
1 teaspoon mustard
275ml/½ pint milk
50g/2oz cashew nuts, toasted
Salt and pepper to taste
50g/2oz Cheddar cheese, grated
2 tablespoons wholemeal
  breadcrumbs
2 tomatoes, sliced
Pinch of parsley

Use a 20cm/8in flan dish, well oiled

Pre-heat oven to 200°C/400°F/Gas Mark 6
Microwave: After 12 minutes transfer to a conventional oven to brown.

---

1 Roll out the pastry and line the flan dish.

---

2 For the filling, boil the macaroni *al dente* and transfer to a bowl. In a pan, lightly sauté the onion, garlic and vegetables in hot butter. Strain, and reserve the juices. Add the flour and mustard to the liquid and form a roux. Pour in the milk. Stir and heat to thicken. Add the macaroni, vegetables, nuts and seasoning. Mix well and pour on to the pastry base. Cover with grated cheese, a sprinkling of breadcrumbs and slices of tomatoes on the top. Finish with some parsley to garnish. Bake for 30 minutes until golden brown.

Variations: Instead of vegetables, use bacon, chicken livers, sweetbreads or any other meats. Turn the savoury into a sweet flan by replacing the vegetables, cheese and seasoning with a little cream, fruits and flavour with rum, vanilla or spices.

Serving suggestion: Serve hot as a first course with a glass of Chianti and a side salad of green lettuce, potatoes and Italian tomatoes. Add a dash of vinaigrette.

Freezing: Will freeze for up to 3 months or keep for 3 days in the fridge.

Basic Savoury Pastry

Makes 450/1lb pastry   Preparation time: 20 minutes

This is a basic savoury pastry for use with many of the recipes which are included in this book. In order to make half this amount simply halve the quantities given.

275g/10oz soft flour
190g/6½oz butter
Pinch of salt
Pinch of mustard
1 egg

1   Blend the flour and the butter together well. Add the salt, mustard and the egg. Mix to form a short pastry.

Freezing: This pastry will keep for up to 3 months sealed in an airtight container and stored in the freezer.

Onion Farm Quiche

Makes 1   Preparation time: 45 minutes   Baking time: 30 minutes

A certain Mrs Forest served the best country quiche I ever ate, which was not surprising since she used fresh farm eggs, milk, cream, butter, cured bacon and onions pulled fresh from her vegetable garden.

For the savoury pastry:
225g/8oz soft flour
150g/5oz butter
Pinch of salt
Pinch of mustard
1 egg

For the filling:
1 large onion, sliced
50g/2oz butter

50g/2oz bacon, chopped
2 eggs
275ml/½ pint milk
50ml/2 fl oz cream
Salt and pepper
½ teaspoon mixed herbs
50g/2oz Cheddar cheese, grated

Use 20cm/8in quiche dish or tin, well oiled

Pre-heat the oven to 200°C/400°F/Gas Mark 6
Microwave: After 12 minutes transfer to a conventional oven to brown.

---

1 For the pastry, blend the flour and butter. Add the salt, mustard and the egg. Mix to form a short pastry. Line a 20cm/8in quiche dish.

---

2 For the filling, fry the onions in the butter with the bacon. Cool and spread over the pastry. Whisk the eggs with the milk, cream and seasonings. Pour onto the quiche base. Finish with a sprinkling of herbs and grated cheese.

---

3 Bake for 30 minutes till set and golden brown.

Variations: Substitute the onion with leeks and add grated Stilton, or a combination of mushrooms, courgettes, tomatoes, beans, etc., plus any variety of meats you choose.

Serving suggestion: Serve cold with salads or hot with French fries and a glass of cider.

Freezing: Will freeze baked for 3 months or keep for 1 week in the fridge.

Pork and Apricot Pie

Makes 1   Preparation time: 35 minutes   Baking time: 45 minutes

Simple Simon would have loved these pies. Tender lean pork laced with the sharpness of apricots, with just enough fat to shorten the pastry.

For the pastry:
450g/1lb Basic Savoury Pastry
  (page 118)

For the filling:
275g/10oz lean pork
100g/4oz lard
25ml/1fl oz water
½ teaspoon salt
¼ teaspoon pepper
Pinch of nutmeg
Pinch of sage
100g/4oz dried apricots, soaked
25g/1oz gelatin
275ml/½ pint stock or water

For the glaze:
1 egg
Pinch of salt

Use an 18cm/7in wide, 7.5cm/3in deep pie dish or tin, well oiled

Pre-heat the oven to 200°C/400°F/Gas Mark 6
Microwave: After 15 minutes transfer to a conventional oven to brown.

---

1   Roll out the pastry and line the pie dish, reserving some pastry for the pie lid.

---

2   Mix the pork, fat, water and seasoning together. Fill the pie with half the pork mixture, then the apricots, and then the remaining pork. Finish off with a few apricots on top.

---

3   For the top of the pie roll out the remaining pastry thinly and enclose the filling. Seal the edges and egg wash the top. Make a hole in the top to allow the air to escape.

---

4   Bake for 45 minutes till crisp and golden brown.

120

5   When cool, pour the gelatin melted in the stock or water through the hole in the top of the pie. This will fill the gaps left by shrinkage of the meat in cooking. Refrigerate till ready to serve.

Variations: Apples, sultanas and oranges all go down well with pork. Try a half pork and half poultry mixture as an alternative. Boiled eggs can be used instead of the fruit.

Serving suggestion: Serve cold with a mixed green salad and yoghurt dressing.

Freezing: Will freeze baked for 3 months or keep for 6 days in the fridge.

Yeovil Egg and Bacon Pie

Makes 1   Preparation time: 35 minutes   Baking time: 35 minutes

Breakfast is always a rush; wouldn't it be nice to eat your eggs and bacon on the way to work? Well, you can! Here they are together in a case of energy-giving pastry.

For the pastry:
225g/8oz Basic Savoury Pastry
  (page 118)
100g/4oz Rough and Puff Pastry
  (page 96)

For the filling:
275g/10oz back bacon, fried
1 tomato

Black pepper
4 eggs

For the glaze:
1 egg
Pinch of salt

Use an 18cm/7in pie dish or tin, well oiled

Pre-heat the oven to 200°C/400°F/Gas Mark 6
Microwave: After 10 minutes transfer to a conventional oven to brown.

---

1   Roll out the savoury pastry and line the pie dish.

---

2   Dice the fried bacon or layer the rashers whole onto the pastry. Slice the tomato and cover the bacon with it. Season. Leaving them whole, crack the eggs and pour over the tomato.

---

3   Roll out the puff pastry thinly and enclose the filling. Seal the edges and egg wash the top. Make a hole for the air to escape.

---

4   Bake for 35 minutes until crisp and golden brown.

Variations: Substitute the bacon and tomato with ham and mushroom, or sausage and baked beans. Or you can use boiled eggs if you prefer.

Serving suggestion: Either eat for breakfast or for lunch.

Freezing: Will freeze baked for 1 month or keep for 4 days in the fridge.

Priory Cheese Soufflés

Makes 12   Preparation time: 35 minutes   Baking time: 20 minutes

Finger food is popular at parties. These soufflés are very light and nutritious and will appeal in particular, to those who wish to lose a little weight!

For the pastry:
450g/1lb Choux Pastry
 (page 104)

For the filling:
100g/4oz curd cheese
100g/4oz butter
100ml/4fl oz milk
2 teaspoons chives, chopped
Pinch of paprika

Use a 30cm/12in baking sheet, well oiled

Pre-heat the oven to 200°C/400°F/Gas Mark 6
Microwave: After 5 minutes transfer to a conventional oven to brown. For best results use the conventional oven only.

---

1   Using a 1cm/½in piping tube, pipe miniature choux buns onto a greased baking sheet, allowing room to expand. Bake in the oven till light and crisp. Cool before filling.

---

2   For the filling, lightly beat the cheese and butter together. Add the milk and stir in the chives and paprika.

---

3   Cut the choux buns in half and spoon or pipe in the filling. Serve immediately.

Variations: Add chopped nuts, seeds or dried fruits as an alternative. Season with garlic, cumin or any other spice to suit your taste.

Serving suggestion: Serve at wine parties as part of a buffet.

Freezing: Will freeze unbaked for 3 months or keep for 6 days in the fridge.

Krac Macs

Makes 16   Preparation time: 25 minutes   Baking time: 20 minutes

A quick and easy snack to make. Children love the crispy, cheesy taste.

For the pastry:
450g/1lb Rough and Puff Pastry
 (page 96)

For the filling:
1 egg (for egg wash)
1 tablespoon yeast extract
100g/4oz Cheddar cheese, grated
100g/4oz sesame seeds

Use a 30cm/12in baking sheet, well oiled

Pre-heat the oven to 200°C/400°F/Gas Mark 6
Microwave: After 5 minutes transfer to a conventional oven to brown. For best results use the conventional oven only.

---

1 Roll out the pastry thinly to a rectangular shape. Egg wash and spread the yeast extract over half the surface. Sprinkle with cheese. Fold over and roll out to 5mm/¼in thick and 15cm/6in long. Cut 5mm/¼in strips and twist each one. Egg wash and dip into sesame seeds. Place onto the baking sheet.

---

2 Bake for 20 minutes until light and crisp.

Variations: Add chopped nuts or seeds. As an alternative, use cream cheese spread thinly with garlic, celery salt, cumin or any spice to suit your taste. Dip into poppy, carraway or fennel seeds to vary the flavour. For mini cheese straws, cut the pastry into 7.5cm/3in strips.

Serving suggestion: Ideal for wine parties with vegetable dips or hot with a savoury fondue.

Freezing: Will freeze for 3 months or will keep for 1 week in a container.

Two-Bite Pizza

Makes 16   Preparation time: 35 minutes   Baking time: 20 minutes

Designed for those who love pizzas — but in miniature. You can choose from a selection of fillings and flavours.

For the base:
450g/1lb Bread Dough (page 24)

For the filling:
1 onion, chopped
1 clove garlic
75ml/3fl oz olive oil

50g/2oz tomato purée
200g/7oz tin tomatoes
1 teaspoon oregano
Salt and pepper
100g/4oz mushrooms, peppers,
  sweetcorn or beans
100g/4oz Mozzarella cheese,
  grated

Use 2 × 30cm/12in baking sheets, well oiled

Pre-heat the oven to 200°C/400°F/Gas Mark 6
Microwave: After 5 minutes transfer to a conventional oven to brown. For best results bake in the conventional oven only.

1   Roll out the dough thinly and cut out 16 circles with a 5cm/2in cutter. Place on the baking sheets and brush with olive oil.

2   To make the filling, sauté the onion and garlic in a little oil. Add the pureé, tomatoes, oregano and seasoning. Bring to the boil and simmer for 20 minutes.

3   Spoon the filling onto the pizza bases. Place a sliced vegetable on top and finish with grated cheese. Allow to prove before baking. Bake for 20 minutes till golden and crisp.

Variations: Instead of bread dough, use puff pastry. The fillings can vary from ham, chicken to meat, seafood and all the many varieties of vegetables.

Serving suggestion: The sort of thing which goes well at buffet parties. You could call them Bits and Pizzas!

Freezing: Will freeze unbaked for 3 months.

Lanark Game Pie

Makes 1   Preparation time: 35 minutes   Baking time: 45 minutes

The strong, distinctive flavours of game meat can be somewhat overpowering. To mellow and tenderise the meat, it can be marinated in red wine, as here. Venison, rabbit, pigeon or any fowl is suitable.

For the pastry:
675g/1lb 8oz Basic Savoury
  Pastry (page 118)

For the filling:
225g/8oz mixed game
125ml/4fl oz red wine
1 tablespoon oil
½ onion
1 clove garlic
50g/2oz dark mushrooms
225g/8oz sausage meat
75g/3oz lard
2 tablespoons breadcrumbs
1 egg
Salt and pepper to taste
½ teaspoon mace
Egg wash
15g/½oz gelatin
100ml/4fl oz water

Use a 20cm/8in deep pie dish, well oiled

Pre-heat the oven to 200°C/400°F/Gas Mark 6
Microwave: After 18 minutes transfer to a conventional oven to brown.

1   Roll out the pastry and line the pie dish.

2   Marinate the game overnight in the wine and oil.

3   For the filling, sauté the onion and garlic in a little oil. Add the mushrooms and transfer to the game meat. Mix all together thoroughly. Add the sausage meat, pork fat, breadcrumbs, egg and seasoning, including the mace, and mix well.

4   Spoon the filling into the pastry base and cover with pastry. Crimp the edges, egg wash and make a hole in the centre for the air to escape.

5   Bake in the oven for 45 minutes till golden in colour. When cool, pour the melted gelatin and water in through the hole in the top to seal the pie.

Variations: For a milder flavour, use chicken, turkey, duck or goose meat. Veal, pork or beef can be used to produce a more traditional pie.

Serving suggestion: Serve hot or cold with Cranberry sauce, or a potato, chive and sour cream salad.

Freezing: This pie will freeze baked for up to 3 months or keep for 7 days in the fridge.

Pâté Butt-Chess

Makes 10   Preparation time: 1 hour   Baking time: 35 minutes

Take a piece of enriched bread dough and enclose a portion of homemade liver pâté. Baked with care, these little delicacies will reward you with tantalising taste sensations.

For the casings:
450g/1lb Butt-Chess dough (page 50)

For the filling:
225g/8oz pigs liver
100ml/4oz green bacon
½ onion
1 clove garlic
25g/1oz butter
2 tablespoons brandy
Salt and pepper
Pinch of mace
Pinch of sage
1 tablespoon blanched almonds,
 chopped
Egg wash
12g/½oz gelatin
100ml/4fl oz water

Use 10 × 5cm/2in fluted patty tins, well oiled

Pre-heat the oven to 220°C/425°F/Gas Mark 7
Microwave: After 10 minutes transfer to a conventional oven to brown.

---

1   Divide the dough into 10 pieces and shape into round balls. Rest for 10 minutes.

---

2   For the filling, lightly cook the liver, bacon, onion and garlic in the butter. Transfer to a bowl and marinate in the brandy for 1 hour.

---

3   Mix together in a blender the liver, bacon, onion and garlic until smooth. Add the seasoning, spice and almonds.

---

4   Roll the dough balls flat. Spoon the filling onto the centre of each and enclose it by pinching to seal in the pâté. Place each into the patty tins, smooth-side up. Prove for 30 minutes. Egg wash the tops.

---

5   Bake in the oven for 35 minutes until golden in colour. When cool, make a hole in the centre and pour the gelatin and water mixture in to fill any gaps.

Variations: Use mushrooms with either chicken, turkey, duck or goose liver to impart a delicate flavour.

Serving suggestion: Serve hot or cold with Cumberland sauce and buttered French beans.

Freezing: Will freeze unbaked for 3 months or keep in the fridge for 3 days.

Marine Seafood Quiche

Makes 1   Preparation time: 35 minutes   Baking time: 35 minutes

Along the coast towards Perranporth in Cornwall, there was a little bistro owned by Louis Master, which served a slice of seafood tart which lingered in my memory, for it was truly exquisite. The memory is fading but the recipe lingers on. Here it is.

For the pastry:
350g/12oz Basic Savoury Pastry
  (page 118)

For the filling:
1 small onion
1 clove of garlic
1 tablespoon olive oil
4 tablespoons tomato purée
½ red pepper

225g/8oz shrimps, prawns and
  mussels
1 teaspoon mint, chopped
1 teaspoon parsley, chopped
Salt and pepper
275ml/½ pint milk
150ml/¼ pint cream
3 eggs
50g/2oz croûtons
50g/2oz cheese, grated

Use a 20cm/8in quiche dish, well oiled

Pre-heat the oven to 200°C/400°F/Gas Mark 6
Microwave: After 12 minutes transfer to a conventional oven to brown.

1   Roll out the pastry and line a quiche dish.

2   For the filling, sauté the onion and the garlic in a little oil. Add the purée, pepper, seafood and herbs. Season to taste. Cook for 1 minute.

3   Spoon the filling onto the quiche. Proceed to mix the milk, cream and eggs. Pour over the filling. Finish with croûtons and a sprinkling of cheese.

4   Bake in the oven for 35 minutes until set and golden.

Variations: Instead of seafood use fresh cuts of fish — sole, halibut, tuna, haddock or salmon. Smoked fish is also suitable, in combination with exotic vegetables. Other fillings include ham, chicken, turkey and the many varieties of vegetables.

Serving suggestions: Serve hot or cold with chilli bean salad and glasses of cool lager. Then you'll share with me my memory of the dish!

Freezing: Will freeze for 3 months or keep for 3 days in the fridge.

Wellington Rolls

Makes 10   Preparation time: 45 minutes   Baking time: 25 minutes

Sausage rolls are a useful snack eaten at picnics, parties and special occasions. On the same principle, and with a tastier filling, these are an alternative and are called Wellington Rolls.

For the pastry:
450g/1lb Rough and Puff Pastry (page 96)

For the filling:
25g/1oz butter
50g/2oz mushrooms, chopped
½ small onion

1 tablespoon breadcrumbs
2 teaspoons parsley, chopped
1 tablespoon white wine
Salt and pepper
175g/6oz Liver Pâté (page 128)
275g/10oz pork or beef sausage meat
Egg wash

Use a 30cm/12in baking sheet, well oiled

Pre-heat the oven to 220°C/425°F/Gas Mark 7
Microwave: After 4 minutes transfer to a conventional oven to brown.

1   Roll out the pastry to 5mm/¼in thickness and 12.5cm/5in width.

2   For the filling, lightly cook in the butter the mushrooms and onion. Add the breadcrumbs, parsley, wine and seasoning. Finally add the pâté and form a paste.

3   Spread the mixture thinly over the pastry allowing a 1cm/½in border all round. Roll out the sausage meat and place in the centre of the pâté. Egg wash the border and fold over. Seal edges and decorate with knife cuts in the top.

4   Cut into 10cm/4in lengths, egg wash the tops and transfer to the baking sheet. Bake for 25 minutes until golden in colour.

Variations: Instead of liver pâté, try a purée of vegetables mixed with an egg to bind. Season with herbs and spices to suit your taste.

Serving suggestion: Serve hot or cold as a finger snack with pickled cucumbers and a glass of rosé wine.

Freezing: Will freeze unbaked for 3 months or keep for 3 days in the fridge.

Spotted Gloucester Pie

Makes 1   Preparation time: 45 minutes   Baking time: 35 minutes

This pie contains iron-packed goodness in the form of liver, bacon and vegetables, surrounded by a piquant sauce. A nice way to eat liver and bacon.

For the pastry:
225g/8oz Basic Savoury Pastry
  (page 118)
225g/8oz Rough and Puff Pastry
  (page 96)

For the filling:
150g/5oz liver, chopped
100g/4oz bacon rashers
25g/1oz butter
50g/2oz white mushrooms,
  chopped
5 small shallots
1 tomato
1 tablespoon brandy
1 tablespoon sultanas
Salt and pepper to taste
1 teaspoon fresh thyme, chopped
Pinch of parsley
50ml/2fl oz cream
Egg wash

Use a 20cm/8in pie dish, well oiled

Pre-heat the oven to 200°C/400°F/Gas Mark 6
Microwave: After 5 minutes transfer to a conventional oven to brown.

1   Roll out the Basic Savoury Pastry and line the tin, reserving the Rough and Puff Pastry for the pie lid.

2   For the filling, lightly cook the liver and bacon in the butter. Line the pastry with half the rashers and cover these with the chopped liver. In the same pan as you cooked the liver and bacon and retaining the meat juices, cook the mushrooms, shallots and tomato. Transfer to the pastry and cover the liver, leaving the juices in the pan. Heat the pan and add the brandy, sultanas, seasoning and herbs and cream. Cover the vegetables with this and finish with the final rashers of bacon.

3 Cover the filling with the pastry lid and crimp edges. Egg wash the top and decorate with pastry leaves. Egg wash.

4 Bake for 35 minutes until golden in colour.

Variations: Instead of liver, try cubes of chicken or pork fillets. Alter the seasonings for a varied taste.

Serving suggestion: Serve hot with puréed swede, black pepper and a tomato and gherkin sauce. Try it with a glass of fine burgundy — a meal worthy of acclaim!

Freezing: Will freeze unbaked for 3 months or keep for 3 days in the fridge.

CHAPTER 6

DOWN THE LANE CAKES AND SPONGES

The term 'cake' is derived from the word 'kaka'. These were small cake-like tea breads made from oats. Variations included buns, pancakes, pikelets and scones.

The change from bread to cake occurred in the eighteenth century when bakers were prohibited by law from making enriched cake breads except on special occasions such as Christmas, Easter, weddings and so on.

They had discovered that by adding large quantities of eggs, sugar and butter to their original dough, and beating it to a light creamy batter, they could produce an aeration that replaced the need for the barm and leaven which had previously given the bread its lift. The introduction of chemical raising agents, such as ammonium carbonate, tartaric acid, bicarbonate of soda and finer milled flours, has since led the way to some of the many regional specialities which survive today. Cake is now a part of our national heritage — a link with the past. To understand the various techniques involved in cakemaking we should look at the four basic mixing methods:

1   The Sponge: Eggs and sugar are mixed to a peak. The flour is then folded in and the mix deposited into tins and baked. Suitable for sponges, Swiss-rolls and madeleines.

2   The Sugar Batter Method: Sugar and fat are beaten to a light cream. The eggs are added in stages. The mixture is well beaten to clear the batter and then finally the flour is folded in and mixed till a smooth clear dough is produced. Suitable for Madeira, Victoria and lightly-fruited cakes.

3   The Flour Batter Method: The fat and part of the flour is creamed together. The eggs and sugar are whisked to a sponge and added to the flour batter. Finally the remaining flour is folded in. Suitable for heavy and light fruit cakes. A stronger flour can be used without fear of toughening. Fruit will not sink, as may occur in the Sugar Batter Method. Eggs will not curdle either.

4   The All-In Method: Just add all the ingredients and cream lightly. To improve the aeration, just add a little baking powder. Suitable for quick cakes.

To balance a cake, these points are worth remembering:

1   The eggs aerate their own weight of flour.

2 Plain cakes will stand more aeration than fruit cakes.

3 25g/1oz of baking powder will aerate 450g/1lb of flour (in excess of eggs).

4 Sugar should be present up to the extent of 20% of the total weight (except sponges).

5 Cornflour will improve texture. Rice flour, ground almonds, etc., count as flour when weighing.

Why Your Cakes May Sink

There are many reasons for this, but a few are that you have used too much egg, baking powder, milk or sugar. Too little flour, insufficient mixing, under-baking or the cake being knocked whilst baking may have the same effect.

When making sponges, make sure all the utensils are grease-free otherwise the sponge will not whip to its maximum, resulting in small volume sponges. Fruit will sink to the bottom if the flour is too soft, if the batter if overmixed or if the fruit is wet and syrupy.

Important points to note: The temperature of the batter should be about 20°C/70°F. Keep the fats and egg warm to avoid curdling. Oven baking temperatures will vary according to the richness and texture of the batter. Rich fruit cakes bake longer in a lower temperature. Light sponges bake quicker in a higher temperature.

If you enjoy cakemaking try one or two recipes in this chapter. You may be surprised at your own skill.

Andy's Dundee Cake

Makes 2   Preparation time: 30 minutes   Baking time: 1 hour 30 minutes

This famous festive treat comes from Scotland. A fruit cake with almonds neatly placed on top and laced with whisky.

225g/8oz butter or margarine
225g/8oz dark brown sugar
275ml/½ pint eggs, beaten and
 warmed
15g/½oz caramel colour
275g/10oz plain flour
25g/1oz ground almonds
½ teaspoon baking powder

450g/1lb sultanas
50g/2oz orange peel
2 tablespoons whisky
½ teaspoon cinnamon
Zest of an orange
Vanilla or almond essence
Almonds

Use 2 × 15cm/6in diameter, 6.5cm/2½in deep cake hoops or tins, oiled and floured, or lined with greaseproof paper. Oval or square shapes are also suitable.

Pre-heat the oven to 180°C/350°F/Gas Mark 4
Microwave: After 20 minutes transfer if preferred to a conventional oven to brown.

---

1 Into the mixing bowl cream the fat and sugar till light and fluffy. In three stages pour in the eggs, beating in continually. Avoid curdling.

---

2 Carefully blend in the caramel, the sifted flour, almonds and baking powder using a spatula or clean hands until all has dispersed. Mix together the fruits, whisky, spice, zest and flavourings and add to the batter. Mix well.

---

3 Weigh 750g/1lb 11oz of the mixture into each hoop or tin. Level off with a dampened hand. Arrange the almonds neatly on the top. Cover with greaseproof paper during baking to prevent burning on top. Remove the paper after 1 hour of baking.

---

4 Bake for 1 hour 30 minutes till light and golden in colour. Check with fingers or a knife to see when it is fully baked. For a shiny surface glaze, while still hot with a mixture of whisky and honey. When baked and cool remove from the tin.

Variations: Add 100g/4oz cherries and omit 100g/4oz sultanas.
Add 50g/2oz chopped almonds instead of peel.
To store the cakes, wrap in greaseproof paper and leave in a cool place to mature.

Freezing: Will freeze for up to 3 months.

No-fat Egg Sponge

Makes 5 sponges   Preparation time: 35 minutes   Baking time: 20 minutes

Only eggs, flour, a little flavour and a lot of attention are required to make sponges that are light as a feather and even more tasty.

275ml/½ pint eggs beaten and
  warmed
Vanilla essence
275g/10oz sugar
275g/10oz soft plain flour

Use 5 × 18cm/7in diameter, 2.5cm/1in deep sponge tins, oiled and floured

Pre-heat the oven to 200°C/400°F/Gas Mark 6
Microwave: After 6 minutes transfer to a conventional oven.

---

1 In a grease-free mixing bowl whisk the eggs, vanilla and sugar to a stiff peak. Carefully blend in the sifted flour using a spatula or clean hands, until all the flour has dispersed.

---

2 Weigh out 175g/6oz of the mixture and deposit into each of the sponge tins. Bake for 20 minutes until light and golden brown in colour.

Secret tip: To improve the whipping of the eggs, make sure all the utensils are clean and oil-free. Once the eggs and sugar have reached their peak, take care not to knock the mixture or overmix when adding the flour. To vary the flavour, add ground nuts, the zest of an orange or lemon, coffee or cocoa powder. Make allowances for these by reducing the flour accordingly.

Serving suggestion: Serve sandwiched with raspberry jam or a variety of flavoured cream. This sponge is suitable for trifles and many other desserts.

Freezing: Will freeze for up to 3 months. Keeps for 1 week in the fridge.

Madeleines

Makes 24   Preparation time: 45 minutes   Baking time: 15—20 minutes

These are popular with children — the tangy speckled coconut coating will keep even the noisiest of offspring quiet... for at least a minute!

150ml/¼ pint eggs, beaten and
  warmed
Few drops vanilla essence
225g/8oz sugar
250g/9oz soft plain flour
15g/½oz baking powder
25ml/1fl oz glycerine
150ml/¼ pint milk

For the coating:
450g/1lb apricot purée, boiled
100g/4oz fine coconut
100g/4oz Fondant Icing
  (page 178)
24 glacé cherries

Use 24 dariole moulds, oiled and floured

Pre-heat the oven to 200°C/400°F/Gas Mark 6
Microwave: After 6 minutes transfer to a conventional oven to brown.

1   In a grease-free mixing bowl whisk the eggs, vanilla and sugar to a stiff peak. Carefully blend in the sifted flour and baking powder using a spatula or clean hands until all the flour is dispersed. Finally add the glycerine and milk.

2   Spoon the mixture into the moulds, filling to ¾ depth.

3   Bake for 15—20 minutes till light and golden in colour.

4   When baked, empty the tins and cool the sponges. Using a fork, dip each one into the boiling apricot purée and cover with coconut. Melt the fondant and pipe a spot on the top of each madeleine. Finish with a glacé cherry.

Variations: Use roasted coconut and finish with coffee fondant icing with a walnut on top. (See Victorian Sandwich, page 150.)

Serving suggestion: Serve as pastries for tea and coffee mornings. This sponge is also suitable for trifles and many other desserts.

Freezing: Will freeze for up to 3 months, or keep for 1 week in the fridge.

M'Lady's Cake

Makes 3 cakes   Preparation time: 25 minutes   Baking time: 40—50 minutes

Before 1914 it was always the fashion to listen to the Palm Court Orchestra at the Grand Hotel, and to enjoy the ritual of tea and cake. And, oh, what cake — even the crumbs taste good!

250g/9oz butter or margarine
350g/12oz caster sugar
350ml/12fl oz eggs, beaten and
  warmed
25g/1oz glycerine

450g/1lb soft plain flour
2 teaspoons baking powder
Zest of a lemon
50g/2oz citron peel

Use 3 × 15cm/6in diameter, 6.5cm/2½in deep cake hoops or tins, oiled and floured, or lined with greaseproof paper

Pre-heat the oven to 190°C/375°F/Gas Mark 5

---

1   Into the mixing bowl cream the fat and the sugar till light and fluffy. In three stages pour in the eggs and glycerine, beating in continually.

---

2   Carefully blend in the sifted flour and baking powder using a spatula or clean hands until all the flour has dispersed. Finally add the lemon zest.

---

3   Weigh out 450g/1lb of the mixture for each of the hoops or tins. Level the tops and finish with a sprinkling of citron peel.

---

4   Bake for 40—50 minutes till light and golden brown. When baked, remove from tins and cool before cutting.

Variations: Add 15g/½oz carraway seeds, or 50g/2oz chopped walnuts or any other nuts, or add 50g/2oz cocoa powder and juice and zest of an orange. Reduce the flour accordingly.

Serving suggestion: Serve slices with glasses of Madeira wine.

Freezing: Will freeze for up to 3 months, or keep for 1 week in airtight container.

Celebration Cake

Makes 2 cakes   Preparation time: 30 minutes   Baking time: 1 hour 50 minutes

The rich, dark-coloured cakes we eat at Christmas, Easter and weddings can all be made from this recipe, given a few variations. Remember, the more fruit, the richer and heavier the cake will be.

225g/8oz butter or margarine
225g/8oz dark brown sugar
275ml/½ pint eggs, beaten and
  warmed
15g/½oz glycerine
275g/10oz plain flour
50g/2oz ground almonds
½ teaspoon baking powder
350g/12oz currants
225g/8oz sultanas
100g/4oz raisins
100g/4oz mixed peel
50g/2oz glacé cherries, chopped
50g/2oz walnuts, chopped
1 tablespoon rum
½ teaspoon cinnamon
½ teaspoon mixed spice
Zest of lemon or orange
Vanilla or almond essence

Use 2 × 15cm/6in diameter, 6.5cm/2½in deep cake hoops or tins, well oiled and floured, or lined with greaseproof paper. Oval or square shapes are also suitable.

Pre-heat the oven to 180°C/350°F/Gas Mark 4
Microwave: After 20 minutes transfer to a conventional oven to brown.

1   Into a mixing bowl cream the fat and the sugar till light and fluffy. In three stages pour in the eggs, beating continually. Avoid curdling.

2   Carefully blend in the glycerine, the sifted flour, almonds and baking powder using a spatula or clean hands until all is dispersed. Mix together the fruits, including mixed peel, nuts, rum, spice and flavourings and add to the batter. Mix well.

3 Weigh out 900g/2lb of the mixture into the tins or hoops. Level the batter with a dampened hand. Cover with greaseproof paper during baking to prevent burning on top. Remove the paper after 1 hour of baking.

4 Bake for 1 hour 50 minutes until light and golden brown in colour. Check with fingers. If surface bounces back when pressed then the cake is ready, or insert a knife which should be clean when removed.

5 When baked, remove from tins and cool before decorating.

Variations: Add 100g/4oz chopped, dried apricots and omit 100g/4oz sultanas.
Add 50g/2oz chopped almonds instead of walnuts.
100g/4oz chopped dates and omit the raisins.
For wedding cakes increase the currants by 100g/4oz and omit 100g/4oz sultanas.
For Simnel Cakes layer the centre with 175g/6oz marzipan and cover the top with 225g/8oz marzipan toasted under the grill.
To store the cakes wrap in greaseproof paper and leave in a cool, dry place to mature. I would recommend at least 6 weeks to improve the quality.

Freezing: Will freeze for up to 3 months.

Country House Cake

Makes 2   Preparation time: 30 minutes   Baking time: 45—55 minutes

Every harvest time, country families celebrate with all kinds of activities. One such activity is the cutting of the Country House Cake — a crumbly textured delight with a hint of nutmeg. A just reward for a bumper crop.

350g/12oz plain soft flour
15g/½oz baking powder
Pinch of salt
100g/4oz butter or margarine
75g/3oz golden syrup
1 large egg
150ml/¼ pint milk
100g/4oz currants
100g/4oz sultanas
75g/3oz mixed peel
1 teaspoon nutmeg
Zest of lemon or orange
50g/2oz demerara sugar

Use 2 × 15cm/6in diameter, 6.5cm/2½in deep cake hoops or tins, oiled and floured, or lined with greaseproof paper. Oval or square shaped tins are also suitable.

Pre-heat the oven to 180°C/350°F/Gas Mark 4
Microwave: After 15 minutes transfer to a conventional oven to brown.

---

1   Into a mixing bowl sieve the flour, baking powder and salt. Rub in the butter. Warm the syrup and mix into the egg and milk. Pour on to dry ingredients and mix well.

---

2   Mix together the fruits, spice and flavourings and add to the batter. Mix till well distributed.

---

3   Weigh 450g/1lb of the mixture into the hoops or tins and level the batter with a dampened hand. Sprinkle demerara sugar over the top.

---

4   Bake for 45—55 minutes till light and golden brown in colour. Insert skewer to test its readiness. The skewer should come out clean if it is done.

---

5   When baked and cool remove from the tin.

Variations: Add 50g/2oz cherries and omit 50g/2oz sultanas.
Add 75g/3oz chopped almonds instead of peel.
Add 100g/4oz raisins and omit 100g/4oz sultanas.
Add sesame seeds to impart a nutty flavour.

Serving suggestion: Serve as often as you like — cut slices and lightly spread
on farm butter with apple or ginger conserve.

Freezing: Will freeze up to 3 months, or keep 2 weeks in a container.

Cotswold Tudor Cake

Makes 3   Preparation time: 20 minutes   Baking time: 55 minutes

A quick way to make a delicious cake. All the ingredients go in together, producing a tender, fruity teatime treat. One slice is never enough!

275g/10oz plain soft flour
½ teaspoon baking powder
Pinch of salt
225g/8oz caster sugar
100g/4oz brown sugar
225g/8oz white shortening

275g/10oz sultanas
Zest of a lemon
1 teaspoon mixed spice
225g/8oz egg
50g/2oz demerara sugar

Use 2 × 450g/1lb loaf tins, oiled and floured, or lined with greaseproof paper. Oval or square shaped tins are also suitable.

Pre-heat the oven to 180°C/350°F/Gas Mark 4
Microwave: After 15 minutes transfer to a conventional oven to brown.

1   Into the mixing bowl sieve the flour, baking powder, salt and sugars, and rub in the shortening. Mix to form a crumble. Add the sultanas, zest and spice.

2   Pour the egg onto the crumble slowly, stirring continuously to form a batter. Mix till well distributed.

3   Weigh out 450g/1lb of the mixture into the loaf tins and level with a dampened hand. Sprinkle demerara sugar over the top. Bake for 55 minutes until golden brown in colour. Insert a skewer to test whether the cake is fully baked. If it is, the skewer will come out cleanly. When baked and cool remove from the tin.

Variations: Add 50g/2oz cherries and omit 50g/2oz sultanas.
Add 75g/3oz chopped almonds or walnuts.
Add 100g/4oz raisins and omit 100g/4oz sultanas.
Add chocolate chips instead of fruit.

Serving suggestion: Serve at tea parties with plenty of jam.

Freezing: Will freeze for up to 3 months. Keeps for 2 weeks in an airtight container.

Top   Yeovil Egg and Bacon Pie (page 122).
Bottom left   Marine Seafood Quiche (page 130).
Bottom right   Wellington Rolls (page 131).

Top right *Highland Almond Cake* (page 148). **Right** *Victorian Sandwich* (page 150).
Centre and bottom left *M'Lady's Cake Variations* (page 139).

Top *Meringue Nests (page 164).* **Centre** *Viennese Mellows (page 161).*
Bottom *Chocolate Walnut Fingers (page 158).*

Top Treasures in the Chest (page 172). **Centre left** *Coconut Candy (page 179).*
Centre right *Dorset Grenadine Fudge (page 177).*
Bottom *Tricia's Truffles (page 175).*

Carisa Cake

The attractive appearance of cherries makes them ideal for cakemaking. From the simplest trifle to the icing on the cake, cherries make the confection look truly appetising.

225g/8oz butter or margarine
225g/8oz caster sugar
275ml/½ pint warm eggs
350g/12oz plain flour
½ teaspoon baking powder

450g/1lb dried glacé cherries
Zest of a lemon
Vanilla or almond essence
50g/2oz citron peel

Use 4× 15cm/6in diameter, 6.5cm/2½in deep cake hoops or tins, oiled and floured, or lined with greaseproof paper. Oval shape is also suitable.

Pre-heat the oven to 180°C/350°F/Gas Mark 4
Microwave: After 15 minutes transfer if preferred to a conventional oven to brown.

---

1   Into a mixing bowl cream the fat and sugar till light and fluffy. In three stages pour in the eggs, beating continually. Avoid curdling.

---

2   Carefully blend in the sifted flour and baking powder using a spatula or clean hands until all is dispersed. Finally add the cherries, lemon zest and flavourings.

---

3   Weigh out 400g/14oz of the mixture into each tin or hoop. Level the batter and finish with citron peel.

---

4   Bake for 45—50 minutes till light and golden brown. Check with fingers. If the surface bounces back when pressed, the cake is ready.

---

5   When baked, remove from the tin and cool before cutting.

Variations: Add 100g/4oz chopped dried apricots and omit 100g/4oz of cherries. Add 50g/2oz chopped walnuts or any other nuts.

Serving suggestion: Serve slices of Carisa Cake after Sunday lunch with glasses of tawny port.

Freezing: Will freeze for up to 3 months. Keeps for 2 weeks in a container.

Ginger Khan Cake

Makes 4   Preparation time: 25 minutes   Baking time: 45 minutes

As winter approaches our attentions turn towards the warmth of the hearth. Ginger cakes take on a new meaning as the cold wind whistles at your door.

75g/3oz butter
75g/3oz white shortening
175g/6oz brown sugar
175g/6oz golden syrup
225g/8oz egg
350g/12oz plain flour

2 teaspoons ground ginger
½ teaspoon bicarbonate of soda
50g/2oz ginger, chopped
Zest of lemon
100g/4oz Fondant Icing
(page 178)

Use 2 × 15cm/6in round, 6.5cm/2½in deep cake tins, oiled and floured, or lined with greaseproof paper. Oval or square shaped tins are also suitable.

Pre-heat the oven to 180°C/350°F/Gas Mark 4
Microwave: After 15 minutes transfer to a conventional oven to brown.

1   Cream the fats, sugar and syrup till light and fluffy. Add the egg in three stages, beating between each addition. Avoid curdling.

2   Sieve the flour, ginger, bicarbonate of soda and blend in. Add the chopped ginger and zest and mix to clear.

3   Weigh out 275g/10oz of the mixture into cake tins. Level the batter with a dampened hand. Bake for 45 minutes until set. Insert the skewer to see if it comes out clean. When baked and cool remove from the tin. Cover tops with a coating of fondant icing.

Variations: Add 50g/2oz cherries or 50g/2oz sultanas.
Add 75g/3oz chopped almonds or walnuts.
Add 100g/4oz raisins or 50g/2oz mixed peel.
Add 50g/2oz chopped stem ginger to the icing for a gingery flavour.

Serving suggestion: Simply serve slices with fresh farm butter and a little honey.

Freezing: Will freeze for up to 3 months, or keep for 2 weeks in an airtight container.

Parky Parkin

Makes 8   Preparation time: 25 minutes   Baking time: 55 minutes

A great favourite in the north of England. Once a week, Mum would bake Parkin and all the lads in the street could count on sampling a chunk.

225g/8oz margarine
225g/8oz brown sugar
450ml/16fl oz golden syrup
1 egg
550g/1lb 4oz medium oatmeal

350g/12oz bread flour
2 teaspoons baking powder
15g/½oz ground ginger
225g/8oz treacle
575ml/1 pint milk

Use 8 × 15cm diameter, 6.5cm/2½in deep cake tins, oiled and floured or lined with greaseproof paper. Oval or square shaped tins are also suitable.

Pre-heat the oven to 180°C/350°F/Gas Mark 4
Microwave: After 15 minutes transfer to a conventional oven to brown.

1   Cream the fat, sugar and syrup till light and fluffy. Add the egg in 2 stages beating between each addition.

2   Sieve the oatmeal, flour, baking powder and ginger and blend into the batter. Dissolve the treacle in the milk and add to the above. Mix to clear.

3   Weigh 350g/12oz of the mixture into the cake tins and level off with a dampened hand.

4   Bake for 55 minutes till set. Insert a skewer. If it withdraws cleanly the cake is ready. When baked, cool and remove from tins.

Variations: Add 100g/4oz cherries or 350g/12oz sultanas.
Add 100g/4oz chopped almonds or walnuts.
Add 175g/6oz raisins and 50g/2oz mixed peel.
Add 100g/4oz chopped stem ginger and 100g/4oz flaked almonds on top.

Serving suggestion: Ideal snack for picnics, these cakes go well with cheese. The sweet ginger contrasts with the savoury tang of Cheddar.

Freezing: Will freeze for up to 3 months, or keep for 2 weeks in an airtight container.

Highland Almond Cake

Makes 5   Preparation time: 25 minutes   Baking time: 45 minutes

The moist almond texture ensures the good-keeping qualities of this tempting cake. To lower the cost, use ground almonds or cake crumbs instead of marzipan. The flavour will also improve with the addition of almond essence.

400g/14oz butter
450g/1lb caster sugar
200g/7oz raw marzipan
150g/5oz honey
400ml/14fl oz eggs, beaten
675g/1lb 8oz soft flour

15g/½oz baking powder
225ml/8fl oz milk

For the topping:
100g/4oz flaked almonds

Use 5 × 15cm/6in diameter, 6.5cm/2½in deep cake tins, oiled and floured or lined with greaseproof paper. Oval or square shaped tins are also suitable.

Pre-heat the oven to 180°C/350°F/Gas Mark 4
Microwave: After 15 minutes transfer if preferred to a conventional oven to brown.

1   Cream the butter, sugar and marzipan together until light and fluffy. Add the honey and the eggs in three stages, beating between each addition.

2   Sieve the flour and baking powder and blend into the batter. Finally add the milk and mix well to clear.

3   Weigh 450g/1lb of the mixture into each cake tin. Level the mixture with a dampened hand. Sprinkle almonds on top.

4   Bake for 45 minutes until set. Insert a skewer to test readiness — skewer should come out clean. When baked, cool and remove from the tins.

Variations: Add 100g/4oz cherries or 350g/12oz sultanas
Add 100g/4oz chopped almonds or walnuts.
Add 175g/6oz raisins and 50g/2oz mixed peel.
You can also cut the cake through the centre and layer with lemon curd.

Serving suggestion: Serve as an after dinner taster with a glass of port and plenty of fresh fruits.

Freezing: Will freeze for up to 3 months, or keep for 2 weeks in an airtight container.

Genoa Cake

Makes 4 cakes   Preparation time: 30 minutes   Baking time: 40—45 minutes

Light fruit cake was the only thing my Uncle Bob would eat on Sunday afternoons. He used to say 'Cake is not cake without plenty of fruit.' Obviously he never tried a slice of mine.

225g/8oz butter or margarine
225g/8oz caster sugar
275ml/½ pint eggs, beaten and
  warmed
275g/10oz soft plain flour
50g/2oz ground almonds
½ teaspoon baking powder

225g/8oz currants
225g/8oz sultanas
175g/6oz glacé cherries
25g/1oz mixed peel, chopped
Zest of a lemon
Vanilla or almond essence
50g/2oz citron peel

Use 4 × 15cm/6in diameter, 6.5cm/2½in deep sponge cake hoops or tins, oiled and floured, or lined with greaseproof paper.

Pre-heat the oven to 180°C/350°F/Gas Mark 4
Microwave: After 15 minutes transfer, if preferred, to a conventional oven to brown.

1   Into the mixing bowl cream the fat and the sugar till light and fluffy. In three stages pour in the eggs, beating continually.

2   Carefully blend in the sifted flour, almonds and baking powder using a spatula or clean hands until all the flour has dispersed. Finally add the mixed fruits, mixed peel, lemon zest and flavouring.

3   Weigh out 450g/1lb of the mixture for each hoop or tin. Level the batter and finish with the citron peel.

4   Bake for 45—50 minutes until light and golden brown. When baked remove from the tins and cool before cutting.

Variations: Add 175g/6oz chopped dried apricots instead of cherries. You could also try adding 50g/2oz chopped walnuts or other nuts.

Serving suggestion: Serve slices with cups of hot, leaf, tea.

Freezing: Will freeze for up to 3 months. Keeps for 2 weeks in a container.

Victorian Sandwich

Queen Victoria enjoyed cake, especially this light, crumbly sponge which is named after her.

225g/8oz soft flour
2 teaspoons baking powder
150g/5oz butter
225g/8oz caster sugar
Pinch of salt
75ml/3fl oz milk
150ml/¼ pint eggs, beaten
Vanilla essence

For the filling:
225g/8oz icing sugar
75g/3oz butter
25ml/1fl oz evaporated milk
Vanilla to flavour
225g/8oz raspberry jam
Icing sugar

Use 5 × 15cm/6in diameter, 2.5cm/1in deep sandwich sponge tins, oiled and floured, or lined with greaseproof paper. Oval or square shaped tins are also suitable.

Pre-heat the oven to 190°C/375°F/Gas Mark 5
Microwave: After 5 minutes transfer if preferred to a conventional oven to brown.

---

1   Make a crumble with the flour, baking powder and butter. Dissolve the sugar and salt in the milk and add to the dry mixture. Mix for 3 minutes. Finally pour in the eggs and vanilla to taste and mix till clear for about 30 seconds.

---

2   Weigh out 175g/6oz of the mixture into the sponge tins and level with a dampened hand. Bake as above till set and golden in colour. Test with a skewer to ensure its readiness — the skewer should come out clean.

---

3   When baked, remove from oven, cool and remove from tins. Meanwhile, cream the icing sugar, butter, evaporated milk and vanilla to a light and smooth buttercream filling.

4   Cut the sponges and sandwich a layer of jam and buttercream between the
    2 halves. Dust with icing sugar.

Variations: *Ryeswick Sandwich:*   Add ½ teaspoon of cinnamon to the flour and
1 tablespoon of rum to the filling.
Cavendish Sponge: Add 1 tablespoon of instant coffee to the flour and 1 tablespoon of Tia-Maria to the filling. Cover with coffee icing.
Cadiz sandwich: Add 100g/4oz chopped almonds or walnuts to the flour.
Jasper sandwich: Add grated orange or lemon peel to the batter. Layer with orange
curd and chocolate buttercream. Finish with chocolate fondant icing on the top.

Freezing: Freezes for up to 3 months, or keep for 2 weeks in an airtight container.

Granary Malt Cake

Makes 3   Preparation time: 25 minutes   Baking time: 45—50 minutes

This is a wholesome cake with the added fibre and goodness of granary flour.

100g/4oz granary flour
100g/4oz soft flour
1 teaspoon baking powder
75g/3oz white shortening
75g/3oz caster sugar
75g/3oz brown sugar
Pinch of salt

150ml/¼ pint eggs, beaten
75g/3oz malt extract
50ml/2fl oz milk
225g/8oz sultanas
100g/4oz chopped dates
50g/2oz wheatgerm

Use 3 × 15cm/6in diameter, 6.5cm/2½in deep cake tins, oiled and floured or lined with greaseproof paper. Oval or square shape tins are also suitable.

Pre-heat the oven to 180°C/350°F/Gas Mark 4
Microwave: After 15 minutes transfer to a conventional oven to brown.

1 Make a crumble with the flours, baking powder, shortening, sugars and salt. Mix in the eggs, malt extract and milk and add to the dry ingredients. Add the fruit and mix for 1 minute till clear. Do not overmix.

2 Weigh out 350g/12oz of the mixture into each cake tin and level with a dampened hand. Sprinkle wheatgerm on the tops.

3 Bake for 45—50 minutes till set and golden in colour. Insert a skewer to test when it is done. The skewer should come out clean. When baked and cool remove from the tin.

Variations: Add walnuts or pecans instead of the dates.
Add 100g/4oz glacé cherries and omit 100g/4oz sultanas.
Add ½ teaspoon mixed spice to the flour.
Add sesame seeds instead of wheatgerm for a nutty flavour.
Instead of granary flour use 100% wholemeal.
Add 2 ripe bananas and 1 tablespoon of rum to the mixture and omit the other fruit if preferred.

Serving suggestion: A breakfast alternative to muesli, and something which can also be eaten as a snack.

Freezing: Will freeze for up to 3 months, or keep for 2 weeks in an airtight container.

Choc-Chip Layer Cake

Makes 2   Preparation time: 25 minutes   Baking time: 45—50 minutes

Chocolate chips suspended in a rich chocolate creation and layered with a melt-on-the-tongue cream filling. Guaranteed to tempt anyone!

200g/7oz soft flour
100g/4oz cocoa powder
425g/15oz caster sugar
Pinch of salt
25g/1oz milk powder
275g/10oz margarine
350ml/12fl oz eggs, beaten
25ml/1fl oz glycerine
200ml/7fl oz water

Vanilla essence
275g/10oz soft flour
20g/¾oz baking powder
225g/8oz chocolate chips

For the filling:
450g/1lb Chocolate Buttercream
 (page 180)
Icing sugar

Use 2 × 30cm/12in square, 7.5cm/3in deep cake tins, oiled and floured or lined with greaseproof paper. Oval or round can tins also be used.

Pre-heat the oven to 180°C/350°F/Gas Mark 4
Microwave: After 10 minutes transfer to a conventional oven to brown.

---

1   Make a crumble with the flour, cocoa, sugar, salt, milk powder and margarine. Mix the eggs, glycerine, water and vanilla together and add to the crumble in three stages. Beat for 5—7 minutes till light and smooth. Blend in the sieved flour and baking powder. Mix in the chocolate chips until well distributed.

---

2   Weigh out 1225g/2lb 10oz of the mixture into each tin and level the batter with a dampened hand. Bake for 45—50 minutes until set and a skewer can be inserted and removed clean.

---

3   When baked and cool, remove from the tins. Cut into layers and spread chocolate buttercream thinly over the cut surfaces. Replace the layers and dust with icing sugar.

Variations: Omit the chocolate chips and add grated orange peel.
Add walnuts or pecans instead of the chocolate.

Serving suggestion: Serve with a long vanilla milkshake.

Freezing: Will freeze for up to 3 months, or keep for 2 weeks in an airtight container.

Edwardian Pecan Cake

Makes 3   Preparation time: 25 minutes   Baking time: 45—50 minutes

The Edwardian era saw the growth in popularity of all manner of cakes. I have adapted this one to suit the present Elizabethan era!

225g/8oz soft flour
2 teaspoons baking powder
225g/8oz white shortening
75g/3oz caster sugar
75g/3oz brown sugar
Pinch of mixed spice

Pinch of salt
225g/8oz sultanas
25g/1oz mixed peel
50g/2oz pecans
1 large egg
100ml/4fl oz milk

Use 3 × 15cm/6in diameter, 6.5cm/2½in deep cake tins, oiled and floured or lined with greaseproof paper. Oval or square shaped tins are also suitable.

Pre-heat the oven to 190°C/375°F/Gas Mark 5
Microwave: After 15 minutes transfer if preferred to a conventional oven to brown.

1   Make a crumble with the flour, baking powder, shortening, sugars, spice and salt. Then add the fruits and pecans. Mix the egg with the milk and add to the dry mixture. Mix well for 1 minute till clear. Do not overmix.

2   Weigh 350g/12oz of the mixture into each tin and level with a dampened hand. Bake for 45—50 minutes until set and golden in colour. Insert a skewer to test. If the skewer comes out clean, it will be done. When baked and cool remove from the tin.

Variations: Add walnuts instead of pecans.
Add sultanas and raisins (half and half) instead of sultanas.
Add 100g/4oz glacé cherries and omit 100g/4oz sultanas.
Add ½ teaspoon cinnamon to the flour.
Add 100g/4oz chopped dates and omit 100g/4oz sultanas.
Add grated lemon peel to the batter.

Serving suggestion: Serve as an Edwardian tea with a lace tablecloth and bone china!

Freezing: Freezes for up to 3 months, or keep for 2 weeks in an airtight container.

CHAPTER 7

OVEN FRESH BITES
AND BISCUITS

The early gingerbreads and biscuits were a mixture of breadcrumbs, spices and honey, made into a paste with ale or claret. This mixture was formed into flat, thin cakes and shaped into animals, letters or gingermen figures, and then dried till hard and brittle.

The plain Biscuit, or Biskuit as it was then called, was a mixture of flour and water. The salt and leaven were omitted and the biscuits were usually baked twice to prolong their life during long arduous sea voyages. The Sea Biskuit and water kept many a sailor from starving being sometimes their only nourishment. Scottish crews were more fortunate, their biskuits being made from oats. This same type of biscuit survives today as oatcakes.

Biscuits have commemorated many a feast day — Easter biscuits were an annual offering, with almonds arranged in the form of a cross to represent the Crucifixion. During the eighteenth century, the practice of beating egg yolks and whites together produced lighter, finer biscuits, in particular almond, sponge and macaroon-type biscuits.

Today biscuits are a multi-million pound industry. We munch through tons of these, never tiring at the many hundred varieties on offer. With increased sales, the trend towards the American cookie is making inroads into the old-fashioned British biscuit market — often with delicious results!

The major points to remember for making good biscuits are:

1   The flour should be soft not strong, and a little cornflour will improve the shortness.
2   Always keep the paste cool or the dough will toughen.
3   Do not overmix or undermix the paste for it will toughen and may be difficult to roll out.
4   For best results, use caster sugar. If the sugar is too coarse it will show up as flecks on the finished product.
5   The two best methods to use are the 'cream-in' or the 'rub-in' method, as both will produce a crisp, short, melt-in-the-mouth sensation.

In 1607 Lord Herbert of Chirbury wrote 'Lest you think that the Country ruder than it is, I have sent you some bread which is a kind of cake...made in no place in England but in Shrewsbury. Measure not my love by substance of it, which is brittle, but by the form of which it is circular, which is the symbol of eternity.'

Sally's Shortbreads

Makes 20   Preparation time: 20 minutes   Baking time: 15—20 minutes

Every New Year a Scottish tradition is to break the bread — or shortbread as we call it. The biscuit structure is short to eat with a flavour that tingles on the taste buds.

500g/1lb 2oz soft flour
25g/1oz cornflour
2 tablespoons ground rice
300g/11oz butter
200g/7oz sugar
1 egg

For the topping:
50g/2oz caster sugar

Use 2 × 30cm/12in baking sheets, well oiled, or lined with greaseproof paper. Special shortbread moulds can be used to produce decorative pieces.

Pre-heat the oven to 200°C/400°F/Gas Mark 6
Microwave: After 5 minutes transfer to a conventional oven to brown.

1   Mix the flour, cornflour and rice together. Cream the butter, sugar and egg for 1 minute and add the dry mix. Blend to form a paste and continue to mix for 1 minute. Do not overmix or the pastry will toughen. Cover with greaseproof paper and leave in the fridge to cool.

2   Lightly dust the table with flour and roll out the pastry to 1cm/½in thickness. Cut to fit the baking sheet and place the whole piece on the sheet allowing room around the edges to expand. With a knife divide the 2 pieces into 20 smaller biscuits but do not cut right through.

3   Bake for 15—20 minutes till golden brown. Dust the tops with caster sugar and cut into portions while still warm.

Variations: Add 100g/4oz choc-chips or chopped walnuts, almonds, pistachios, currants, glacé cherries, coconut or various seeds.

Serving suggestion: Serve plain and celebrate the New Year with a dram of whisky.

Freezing: Will freeze for up to 3 months, or keep for 3 weeks in a container.

Cats' Tails

Makes 40   Preparation time: 20 minutes   Baking time: 15 minutes

To decorate a special icecream dessert, why not try placing these long delicate biscuits into the sweet, and watch your guests eagerly nibble their way through the crispy buttery delights.

225g/8oz butter
225g/8oz caster sugar
175ml/6fl oz egg whites
275g/10oz soft flour
Vanilla essence
Icing sugar

Use 4 × 30cm/12in square baking sheets, well oiled and floured

Pre-heat the oven to 200°C/400°F/Gas Mark 6
Microwave: After 4 minutes transfer to a conventional oven to brown.

---

1   Cream the butter and sugar till light. Add the egg whites and mix to clear the batter. Finally blend in the flour and vanilla essence.

---

2   Use a plain 5mm/¼in tube and pipe long finger biscuits onto the baking sheets, allowing room to expand.

---

3   Bake for 15 minutes until golden brown. Dust the top with icing sugar or leave plain.

Variations: Flavour the mixture with orange or lemon or cinnamon.

Serving suggestion: Serve plain or as a decoration with icecreams.

Freezing: Will freeze for up to 3 months or keep for 3 weeks in an airtight container.

Chocolate Walnut Fingers

Makes 40   Preparation time: 20 minutes   Baking time: 15 minutes

A light chocolate biscuit that melts in the mouth, is easy to make and will add extra appeal to all mid-morning munchers.

275g/10oz butter
150g/5oz icing sugar
1 egg
350g/12oz soft flour
40g/1½oz cocoa powder
100g/4oz walnuts, chopped
Vanilla essence

For the filling:
100g/4oz raspberry jam
Icing sugar

Use 4 × 30cm/12in square baking sheets, oiled and floured

Pre-heat the oven to 190°C/375°F/Gas Mark 5
Microwave: After 4 minutes transfer to a conventional oven to brown.

---

1   Cream the butter and sugar till light. Add the egg and mix to a clear batter. Finally mix in the sieved flour, cocoa, walnuts and vanilla essence.

---

2   Use a 5mm/¼in star tube and pipe long finger or whirl biscuits onto the baking sheets allowing room to expand.

---

3   Bake for 15 minutes till firm to the touch. When cool, sandwich with raspberry jam and finish with a dusting of icing sugar.

Variations: Sandwich with different flavoured jams or buttercream. As a dessert, fill with whipped cream topped with fresh strawberries. Instead of cocoa, add ½ teaspoon of mixed spice or cinnamon, ginger or coffee.

Serving suggestion: Serve plain as a biscuit or sandwiched as a dessert with fresh fruits.

Freezing: Will freeze for up to 3 months, or keep for 3 weeks in an airtight container.

Almondettes

Makes 20   Preparation time: 20 minutes   Baking time: 15 minutes

After dinner one often partakes of a little conversation. What more to stimulate the chat than a plateful of nutty, chewy Almondettes?

150g/5oz butter
150g/5oz caster sugar
25g/1oz honey
50g/2oz whipped cream
75g/3oz flaked almonds
50g/2oz mixed peel

25g/1oz flour
Vanilla essence

For the coating:
225g/8oz chocolate, melted

Use 4 × 30cm/12in square baking sheets, oiled and floured

Pre-heat the oven to 190°C/375°F/Gas Mark 5
Microwave: After 3 minutes transfer to a conventional oven to brown.

---

1   Boil the butter, sugar and honey to 120°C/248°F. Add the cream and remove from the heat to stir in the almonds, peel, flour and vanilla.

---

2   Spoon small mounds (25g/1oz) of the mixture onto the baking sheets allowing plenty of room to expand all around.

---

3   Bake for 15 minutes till golden in colour. When baked and cold, cover the smooth side with melted chocolate. When nearly set, score patterns with a fork and leave to set hard before serving.

Variations: Use hazelnuts, walnuts, pecans, peanuts or any other nuts. Or add currants, glacé cherries or sesame seeds.
Florentinas: Line a 30cm/12in baking sheet with pastry. Spread the almondette mixture over it and bake as above. Cut into squares and dip the corners into melted chocolate.

Serving suggestion: Serve as a decoration on gateaux, pastries, trifles, icecreams or as a petit four.

Freezing: Will freeze for up to 3 months, or keep for 3 weeks in an airtight container.

Marlborough Munchies

Makes 35   Preparation time: 20 minutes   Baking time: 25—30 minutes

The crispy crunchy taste of munchies makes them absolutely scrumptious with oats and nuts. You can start the day the healthy way.

450g/1lb white shortening
150g/5oz golden syrup
275g/10oz brown sugar
675g/1lb 8oz rolled oats
450g/1lb flaked almonds
50g/2oz sesame seeds

Use a 30cm/12in square, 4.5cm/2in deep baking tray, oiled

Pre-heat the oven to 190°C/375°F/Gas Mark 5
Microwave: After 5 minutes transfer to a conventional oven to brown.

1   Boil the shortening, syrup and sugar. Remove from the heat and add the oats, nuts and sesame seeds. Mix to a crumbly consistency. Transfer the mixture to a greased baking tray and level it out.

2   Bake for 25—30 minutes till golden. When baked and cool divide into 35 portions.

Variations: Add 100g/4oz currants, peel or any dried fruit. Use flaked hazelnuts, chopped walnuts, pecans, peanuts or any other nuts.

Serving suggestion: Serve as a snack at any time. Goes well with cheese and fresh fruit.

Freezing: Will freeze for up to 3 months, or keep for 2 weeks in an airtight container.

Viennese Mellows

Makes 12   Preparation time: 20 minutes   Baking time: 15—25 minutes

This must surely be the lightest pastry you can make, whipped up to perfection with just a very few ingredients.

225g/8oz butter
Few drops vanilla
50g/2oz icing sugar
225g/8oz soft flour

For the topping
Icing sugar
50g/2oz glacé cherries, halved

Use 12 × 50g/2oz paper cases or patty tins, well oiled. Make sure the paper cases are supported by metal cases, otherwise the filling might overflow during baking.

Pre-heat the oven to 200°C/400°F/Gas Mark 6
Microwave: After 4 minutes transfer to a conventional oven to brown.

---

1   Cream the butter, vanilla and sugar to a light fluffy consistency. Add half the flour and beat till light and airy. Scrape around the edges of the bowl and finally add the other half of the flour. Beat till light.

---

2   Using a 1cm/½in star tube and Savoy bag, pipe a spiral effect into each case. Finish with a slight indent in the centre and place half a cherry in the middle. Transfer to the baking sheet.

---

3   Bake for 15—25 minutes till golden in colour. When baked and cool dust with icing sugar.

Variations: Apricot jam can be used instead of cherries, or sprinkle with flaked nuts. Add 50g/2oz currants, peel or any dried fruit to the mixture, but use a plain tube to pipe. Another idea is to add 25g/1oz cocoa powder and omit 25g/1oz flour. For a chocolate flavour, add chocolate chips. Can be piped on short pastry cases or tops of fruit flans and pies, eg apple, mincemeat, Bakewell, etc.

Serving suggestion: Serve as a teatime surprise.

Freezing: Will freeze for up to 3 months. Keeps for 1 week in an airtight tin.

Ratafia Biscuits

Makes 32   Preparation time: 20 minutes   Baking time: 15—25 minutes

A dessert biscuit made with ground almonds and egg whites piped on to wafer paper and finished with whole almonds.

225g/8oz granulated sugar
100g/4oz ground almonds
1 tablespoon ground rice
100g/4oz egg whites
50g/2oz whole almonds, peeled
4 sheets wafer paper (rice paper)

Use 2 × 30cm/12in baking sheets, well oiled and floured or lined with rice paper

Pre-heat the oven to 190°C/375°F/Gas Mark 5
Microwave: After 4 minutes transfer to a conventional oven to brown.

---

1   Blend together the sugar, almonds and rice. Add the egg whites and beat for 2 minutes.

---

2   Use a 5mm/¼in plain tube and Savoy bag. Pipe 1cm/½in button-size biscuits onto wafer paper, 5cm/2in apart. Finish with a whole almond on top.

---

3   Bake for 15—25 minutes till golden in colour. When baked, serve plain or sandwich 2 together with apricot jam.

Variations: Sprinkle with nibbed almonds, walnuts or a diamond-shaped angelica with a half cherry in the centre. Sandwich with various jams and flavoured buttercreams. As a finish, dip half in melted chocolate.

Serving suggestion: Serve as a plain, after dinner, petit four and as a decoration for trifles, icecreams and various desserts.

Freezing: Will freeze for up to 3 months or keep for 3 weeks in a container.

Ko Ko Rocks

Makes 30   Preparation time: 25 minutes   Baking time: 25—30 minutes

A white toasted coral-like confection, the coconut mingling in the air pockets of whipped-up meringue.

350g/12oz granulated sugar
50ml/2fl oz water
150ml/¼ pint egg whites, beaten
25g/1oz flour
25g/1oz fine orange peel,
  chopped

Use 2 × 30cm/12in square baking sheets, oiled and floured or lined with rice paper

Pre-heat the oven to 140°C/275°F/Gas Mark 1
Microwave: After 4 minutes transfer to a conventional oven to brown.

---

1   In a saucepan, boil the sugar and water for 3 minutes. Meanwhile in a grease-free bowl, whisk the egg whites to a soft peak. Slowly pour in the hot sugar syrup, whisking all the time to a stiff peak. Carefully blend in the flour and peel.

---

2   Use a 5mm/¼in plain tube and Savoy bag. Pipe 7.5cm/3in discs onto the wafer paper, 5cm/2in apart. Finish with a sprinkling of coconut on top.

---

3   Bake in a low oven till dry and then toast in a hot oven to brown. When baked, serve plain or dipped in melted chocolate.

Variations: Use ground hazelnuts or almonds instead of coconut. Decorate with cherry halves or sprinkle nibbed almonds, walnuts, etc. on the top.

Serving suggestion: Serve as a base for icecream, sorbets, yoghurt or on its own as a late afternoon nibble.

Freezing: Has a tendency to disintegrate and is therefore not recommended for freezing but will keep for up to 2 weeks in an airtight container.

Meringue Nests

Makes 30   Preparation time: 25 minutes   Baking time: 2 hours

Light white clouds of air-filled meringue, piped into spirals and dried — the ultimate base for mouth-watering sweet creations.

150ml/¼ pint egg whites, beaten
275g/10oz caster sugar

Use 2 × 30cm/12in square baking sheets, oiled and floured or lined with silicon paper

Pre-heat the oven to 100°C/200°F/Gas Mark low
Microwave: After 4 minutes on low setting transfer to the conventional oven to dry out.

---

1 In a grease-free bowl, whisk the egg whites and half the sugar to a stiff peak. Slowly pour in the remainder of the sugar, whisking all the time, again to a stiff peak.

---

2 Use a 5mm/¼in star tube and Savoy bag. Pipe onto silicon paper 9cm/3½in discs and then pipe a circle on the outer edge to form the nests.

---

3 Bake in a low oven till dry. When baked store until required.

Variations: Colour and flavour meringue nests with strawberry, lemon, chocolate, coffee, etc. to suit the filling. Instead of nests, pipe shells, fingers, large bases for Pavlovas or even swans, using a template for accuracy. Meringue Chantilly can also be made, sandwich shells with vanilla icecream topped with whipped cream and a cherry. Serve as a sweet.

Serving suggestion: Serve as a base for icecream, sorbets, yoghurt filled with fresh fruits (eg strawberries, raspberries, kiwifruit, pineapple or hot blackcurrant sauce poured over icecream). These dream desserts are very popular in the summer.

Freezing: Has a tendency to disintegrate and not recommended for freezing. Will keep for weeks in an airtight container.

Japanese Crunchies

Makes 12   Preparation time: 25 minutes   Baking time: 20—30 minutes

Egg whites whipped up to a foam, speckled with ground hazelnuts and piped out to form light buttons of nutty flavoured crunchiness.

150ml/¼ pint egg whites
175g/6oz caster sugar
75g/3oz ground hazelnuts
75g/3oz nibbed hazelnuts
25g/1oz flour

Use 2 × 30cm/12in square baking sheets, oiled and floured, or lined with silicon paper

Pre-heat the oven to 180°C/350°F/Gas Mark 4
Microwave: After 4 minutes on low transfer to the conventional oven to dry out.

---

1   In a grease-free bowl, whisk the egg whites and half the sugar to a stiff peak. Sieve the hazelnuts, flour and remainder of sugar. Carefully blend into the meringue until clear.

---

2   Use a 5mm/¼in plain tube and Savoy bag. Pipe onto silicon paper 5cm/2in round shells. Sprinkle with nibbed almonds.

---

3   Bake for 20—30 minutes till dry. When baked remove from paper and store till required.

Variations: Colour and flavour Buttercream (page 180) with one of these: chocolate, praline, almond, coffee, lime, mint. Sandwich two shells with any of these fillings and finish with spirals of thin, melted chocolate. Place each into a paper case and serve. The Japanese mixture will also make good gateaux bases using fresh cream for the filling. Use a template for accuracy.

Serving suggestions: Serve as Mandarin Fergie: on a 20cm/8in round base, pipe whipped cream, then a layer of mandarins and cover with a meringue base. Pipe whirls of whipped cream around the border and fill centre with a mixture of whipped cream, rum and chestnut purée piped out using a plain tube to resemble spaghetti. Finish decorating the border with mandarins and flaked chocolate.

Freezing: Has a tendency to disintegrate but will freeze or keep in the fridge for 3 days.

Shrewsbury Biscuits

Makes 24   Preparation time: 20 minutes   Baking time: 15—25 minutes

Usually these biscuits are made at Easter. This year why not use a heart-shaped cutter and turn them into Valentine Heart biscuits? You could pipe your true love's name in icing for a romantic treat.

225g/8oz soft flour
Pinch of baking powder
150g/5oz butter
150g/5oz sugar
½ teaspoon cinnamon
1 egg

For the glaze:
1 egg
50g/2oz caster sugar
Egg wash

Use 2 × 30cm/12in square baking sheets, well oiled, or lined with greaseproof paper

Pre-heat the oven to 200°C/400°F/Gas Mark 6
Microwave: After 4 minutes transfer to a conventional oven to brown.

1   Rub in the flour, baking powder and butter to form a crumble. Mix the sugar, cinnamon and the egg and add to the crumble. Mix to a pliable dough. Rest the pastry in the fridge till required.

2   On a lightly floured table, roll out the pastry to a thickness of 5mm/¼in. Using a 10cm/4in fluted or heart-shaped cutter, cut out the biscuits and place onto greased baking sheets, allowing room to expand.

3   Bake for 15—25 minutes till golden in colour. When baked egg wash, and when cool, dust with caster or icing sugar.

Variations: To the basic mix, add 50g/2oz currants or fine coconut, chopped walnuts, almonds, mixed peel, angelica or sesame seeds. Use wholemeal flour instead of white for a nutty and nutritious taste. To decorate, dip the biscuits in any of the above before baking. Place half a cherry in the centre of the Valentine hearts for extra appeal. Another variation is to add 25g/1oz cocoa powder and omit 25g/1oz flour. For chocolate flavour also add chocolate chips.

Serving suggestion: Serve instead of shop bought biscuits. You'll be instantly 'mesmerised' into submission!

Freezing: Will freeze for up to 3 months, or keep for 2 weeks in an airtight container.

CHAPTER 8
DREAMY DESSERTS, SWEETS AND CANDIES

Sugar is not a new product. Over 2000 years ago the Chinese were enjoying a sweet type of cake made with soya flour. The use of cane sugar began to spread across Europe. Honey was the main sweetener up to this time and was used extensively in almond, nut and sweetmeat concoctions. Being sweet and good to eat, sugar found its way into exotic mystical potions and remedies. Even today many medicines contain sugar to help the medicines go down.

If the first and second courses of a meal often tend to feel like a bit of a chore, patience can be rewarded by the creation, presentation and sheer temptation of the dessert, strictly speaking, unnecessary to the diet but so important for the enjoyment of a successful meal.

The dessert evolved from a collection of dishes, both savoury and sweet. These were arranged on the table for people to help themselves. All types of puddings and sweetmeats were eaten along with the meat, fish and game. In the nineteenth century, meals became more defined. Each section of the meal was a separate course. Hence the need for something sweet to finish off the meal. 'Dessert' (from the French word 'desservir', meaning to clear the table) became more elaborate. Fruits, ices, fancy gateaux, preserves and candies were all introduced.

The sweet course today is often concerned with a more healthy approach to eating and so yoghurts, fresh fruit, compôtes and sorbets have to some extent replaced the heavier, steamed puddings.

Trifle Treat

Makes 1   Preparation time: 20 minutes   Baking time: Nil

The classic trifle has changed little since its introduction over 100 years ago. Today jelly and custard versions are more popular than the cream and macaroon varieties used in the eighteenth century. This recipe combines both and produces a real Trifle Treat.

100g/4oz Sponge Cake or Sponge
  Base (page 137)
100g/4oz raspberry jam
100g/4oz crushed Ratafia
  Biscuits (page 162)
75ml/3fl oz sherry
50ml/2fl oz brandy
A little fruit syrup
225g/8oz whipped cream

For the topping:
275ml/½ pint milk
25g/1oz sugar
4 egg yolks
Vanilla essence

For the decoration:
50g/2oz cherries
25g/1oz angelica diamonds
Ratafia Biscuits (page 162)
Flaked almonds, toasted

Use a trifle dish

1   Sandwich a sponge base with jam and line the trifle dish with it. Sprinkle on crushed biscuits. Make a syrup with the sherry, brandy and fruit juice. Soak the sponge base and leave to mature.

2   For the custard topping, boil the milk. Dissolve the sugar in the egg yolks and stir into the milk until the custard thickens. Add the vanilla (a saucepan will prevent burning.) Pour the custard over the sponge and leave to cool.

3   Whip the cream and pipe whirls around the edge, finishing in the centre. Decorate with cherries, angelica, ratafias and flaked nuts.

4   Place in the fridge till ready to serve.

Variations: Instead of sherry and brandy try a mixture of port/rum and wine/kirsch. Use flavoured jelly instead of syrup.
Black Forest Trifle: Substitute vanilla sponge with chocolate sponge sandwiched with cherry pie filling and soaked in kirsch. Cover with chocolate custard and finish with whipped cream, cherries, flaked almonds and chocolate shavings.

Serving suggestion: Serve as a dessert straight from the fridge.

Freezing: Will freeze for 1 month or keep refrigerated for 3 days.

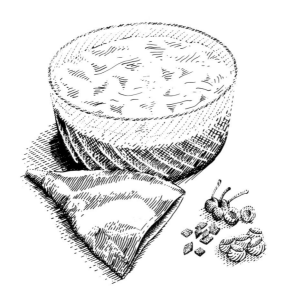

Hub-a-Bub

Makes 2   Preparation time: 25 minutes   Baking time: Nil

A cream dessert presented in a glass coupe shows a layer of jelly floating between liqueur-rich cream.

275ml/½ pint double cream
25g/1oz sugar
Zest and juice of a lemon
50ml/2fl oz sherry
50ml/2fl oz Drambuie
100g/4oz lime jelly, chopped

For the decoration:
Ratafia (page 162) or Cats' Tails
  Biscuits (page 157)

Use 2 glass coupe or dessert dishes

---

1   Whisk the cream to a stiff peak. Mix the sugar, lemon, sherry and Drambuie to a syrup and fold into the cream. Half fill the glasses with this mixture and then add a layer of chopped jelly. Cover with the remaining cream. Finish with a few Ratafias or Cats' Tails arranged neatly on top.

---

2   Place in the fridge until ready to serve.

Variations: Instead of sherry and Drambuie try a mixture taken from the following; cider/brandy; port/rum; wine/kirsch. Omit the jelly for currants or cherries. You could also try raspberries, kiwifruit, apples, etc. Finish with a sprinkling of toasted nuts or flaked chocolate.

Serving suggestion: Serve as a dessert straight from the fridge

Freezing: Will not freeze satisfactorily but will refrigerate for 2 days.

Devils on Fire

Pancakes are a great favourite on Shrove Tuesday but why not throughout the year? Made with a butterscotch sauce and a filling of blackcurrants they make an ideal 'any-time' treat!

50g/2oz butter
25g/1oz caster sugar
1 teaspoon ground almonds
75ml/3fl oz whisky
6 Pikelets or Pancakes (page 76)
100g/4oz blackcurrants (or pie
  filling)
100g/4oz whipped cream
Flaked almonds, toasted

Use 2 dessert dishes

---

1   Melt the butter in a pan and add the sugar. Cook until the mixture turns to a caramel. Add the ground almonds and finally the whisky.

---

2   Take the dessert dishes and place 3 Pikelets into each. Layer with hot blackcurrants or use them cold and microwave for 2 minutes.

---

3   Pour hot butterscotch over the Pikelets plus a little more whisky. Finish with rosettes of fresh whipped cream and a sprinkling of toasted almonds. Serve immediately.

Variations: Hot cherries and brandy make a delicious alternative to blackcurrants. Serve with fresh yoghurt and toasted sesame seeds.
Carribean Sunrise: Use a selection of sliced tropical fruits such as mango, paw paw, pineapple, banana etc. Use the juice of a lime and rum instead of whisky. Finish with coffee-flavoured whipped cream and toasted desiccated coconut.

Serving suggestion: Serve hot or cold as a dessert.

Freezing: Pikelets will freeze for up to 3 months.

Treasures in the Chest

Makes 4   Preparation time: 25 minutes   Baking time: Nil

A cocktail dessert full of hidden treasures. The smooth velvet chocolate sauce buried beneath a layer of crushed meringue and mountains of chestnut cream speckled with flakes of chocolate.

For the sauce:
50g/2oz chocolate, melted
150ml/¼ pint water
15g/½oz butter
25g/1oz cream
4 crushed meringue shells

For the topping:
350g/12oz whipped cream
50g/2oz chestnut purée
25g/1oz sugar
50g/2oz chocolate flakes
25g/1oz gelatin
25ml/2 tablespoons rum
Chestnuts, roasted and grated
Chocolate, grated

Use 4 tall glass dessert dishes

---

1   For the sauce melt the chocolate in a pan and add the water, butter and cream. Stir till smooth, cool and pour into the glasses till quarter full. Place a layer of crushed meringue shells over the sauce.

---

2   For the topping, blend together the whipped cream, chestnut purée, sugar and chocolate flakes. Dissolve the gelatin and rum in warm water and add to the cream mixture. Fill each glass to the top. Finish with a rosette of piped cream, decorated with grated roast chestnuts and chocolate. Chill before serving.

Variations: *Conil's Parfait:* Use puréed raspberries in the base and cover with crushed Ratafia biscuits (page 162). Top with a cream filling of chopped stem ginger, chopped or ground roast hazelnuts and finish with whole raspberries and Cats' Tails (page 157). Or use fresh yoghurt and toasted sesame seeds. Serve as a cold dish.

Gulliver's Pudding

Makes 1   Preparation time: 35 minutes   Baking time: 45 minutes

One way to utilise leftover bread is in a pudding. A custard can be made which soaks into the bread together with a mixture of fruit and spices.

1 small sliced Tea Bread
  (page 46)
100g/4oz butter, melted
50g/2oz mixed dried fruits
50g/2oz dates, chopped
50g/2oz walnuts, chopped
275ml/½ pint milk
2 eggs
25g/1oz sugar
Vanilla essence
1 tablespoon rum
Pince of nutmeg or mixed spice

Use a square pudding dish (2 litres/4 pints) well oiled

Pre-heat the oven to 180°C/350°F/Gas Mark 4
Microwave: For 5 minutes and then transfer to a conventional oven to brown.

---

1   Cut slices of the bread and dip in the melted butter. Arrange the pieces around the base of the dish and sprinkle fruits and nuts over. Cover with another layer of teabread and fruits.

---

2   Mix the milk, eggs, sugar and vanilla and rum. Pour this over the bread and sprinkle nutmeg on the top. Leave to soak before baking as above. When baked serve hot onto dessert dishes.

Variations: Use wholemeal bread and honey to sweeten the pudding. Alternate the fruits using dried apples, apricot, peaches, prunes or figs. Sprinkle dark brown sugar on top and serve.

Serving suggestion: Serve hot or cold as a dessert with maple syrup and topped with a scoop of whipped cream.

Freezing: Freezes for up to 3 months or refrigerates for 3 days. For best results, eat on the day of making.

Georgian Pudding

Serves 6   Preparation time: 45 minutes   Baking time: 45 minutes

Puddings were, until the late seventeenth century, savoury dishes only. As sugars and fruits were introduced to Britain from abroad, puddings increased in popularity. George I set the pattern as 'the pudding-eating monarch'. Today we prefer lighter sweets — this recipe is an example of a pudding that looks light and is delightful to eat.

75g/3oz butter
75g/3oz white flour
225ml/8fl oz milk, hot
3 egg yolks and whites
75g/3oz sugar

Pinch of salt
Vanilla essence
75g/3oz prunes, stoned and
  chopped

Use 6 × 100g/4oz individual pudding moulds or a large pudding basin, well oiled

Pre-heat the oven to 200°C/400°F/Gas Mark 6
Microwave: 6 minutes and then transfer to the conventional oven to brown.

---

1   Cream the butter and add the flour. Pour in the hot milk and stir till smooth. Transfer to the stove and dry slightly. Remove from the heat and add the egg yolks, sugar, salt and vanilla. Mix to a batter.

---

2   Whisk the egg whites to a stiff peak and fold into the batter. Add the prunes and mix to clear. Pour into the greased and sugared moulds up to three-quarters full. Transfer to a deep tray which is half-filled with water. Bake for 45 minutes until light and golden.

---

3   When baked, remove from the moulds and serve hot with a custard sauce.

Variations: Use currants, raisins, sultanas or any dried fruit. Instead of fruits, spoon any flavoured jam or syrup into the bottom of each mould. Pour the sponge batter on the top and bake as above. For chocolate puddings add 25g/1oz cocoa powder and omit 25g/1oz flour. Serve with chocolate sauce.

Serving suggestion: Serve hot as a dessert with golden syrup and custard sauce.

Freezing: Freeze baked for up to 3 months. For best results eat on the day of baking.

Tricia's Truffles

Makes 1225g/2½lb truffles   Preparation time: 45 minutes   Baking time: Nil

A simple confection to make, this is a mixture of chocolate and cream which produces a rich base. It can be enhanced with many flavours — liqueurs, nuts or fruits.

225ml/8fl oz dairy cream
500g/1lb 2oz chocolate, plain or
 milk
25g/1oz butter
1 tablespoon rum
225g/8oz chocolate, melted
225g/8oz chocolate vermicelli

Microwave: For 1 minute to melt the chocolate.

1 In a saucepan, boil the cream and remove from the heat. Add the chopped chocolate, butter and rum. Stir until smooth. Pour into a bowl and cool. When set beat for 1 minute.

2 Using a 5mm/¼in plain tube and savoy bag, pipe long ropes onto greaseproof paper. Cut into 1cm/½in pieces. Roll up into balls. Dip each ball into the melted chocolate and cover with vermicelli. Place the truffles into the paper cases.

Variations: Instead of rum, try brandy, Grand Marnier, Tia Maria etc. Use various chopped nuts or crystallised fruits to vary the flavours, Try covering the truffles with white chocolate, or leave them plain, or coat them in toasted cake crumbs, icing sugar or cocoa powder.

Serving suggestion: Serve after dinner as petits fours, or have a nibble whenever they take your fancy! As a gift, pack them in decorative boxes. They will always be appreciated on birthdays or other special occasions.

Freezing: Truffles do not freeze well but will keep for up to a month stored in a cool place.

Peppermint Pleasers

Makes 1kg/2lb peppermints   Preparation time: 25 minutes   Baking time: Nil

Smooth fondant buttons full of minty flavour and dipped in plain chocolate.

225g/8oz Fondant Icing
   (page 178)
225g/8oz sugar, granulated
225g/8oz icing sugar
1 teaspoon peppermint essence
225g/8oz chocolate, melted

Microwave: 1 minute to melt the chocolate

---

1   In a saucepan, melt the fondant and add the sugars and peppermint essence. Stir to a temperature of 50°C/125°F.

---

2   Using a 5mm ¼ in plain tube and Savoy bag, pipe 2.5cm/1in buttons onto oiled greaseproof paper. When set, dip half the peppermint into the melted chocolate and allow to set.

Variations: Instead of peppermint, try orange, lemon, cherry, pineapple or lime. Use various chopped nuts or crystallised fruits to vary the flavours.

Serving suggestion: Serve after dinner as a refreshing end to a meal.

Freezing: Do not freeze well but will store for up to 3 months in an airtight container.

Dorset Grenadine Fudge

Makes 1kg/2lb   Preparation time: 35 minutes   Baking time: Nil

Whenever I go down to Dorset I always head straight for the nearest fudge shop as this chewy, creamy confectionery has always been my favourite. I remember at nine years of age getting through 25 varieties! Here is one flavour to get you addicted.

225g/8oz dairy cream
225g/8oz evaporated milk,
  unsweetened
50g/2oz butter
450g/1lb caster sugar
25g/1oz glucose
25g/1oz grenadine
Vanilla essence

1   In a saucepan, melt the cream, milk, butter and add the sugar and glucose. Boil the mixture to 120°C/248°F stirring all the time to prevent burning. Add the grenadine and vanilla essence and stir well.

2   Pour the fudge mix into a well oiled tray or tin. Allow to cool before cutting.

Variations: Add chopped nuts, fruits, etc. or flavour with coffee, strawberry, cherry, rum, peppermint, etc.

Serving suggestion: Serve an assortment at Christmas or after a dinner party.

Freezing: Does not freeze well but keeps for 3 months in an airtight container.

Fondant Icing

Makes 675g/1½lb   Preparation time: 25 minutes   Baking time: Nil

This fondant can be used on all cakes and pastries, including many in this book. The smooth velvety surface produces a delicious coating that all children love.

450g/1lb granulated sugar
50g/2oz glucose
150ml/¼ pint water

1   In a saucepan melt the sugar and glucose in the water. Boil the mixture to 110°C/240°F.

2   Pour the boiling sugar onto an oiled marble slab or tray. Use 4 oiled metal bars on the table top to prevent the mixture flowing. Cool to 40°C/100°F and then commence agitating the sugar with a spatula till it turns to a smooth, white icing. Store in a plastic bag or an airtight container.

To Use: Take a little fondant and melt to finger heat in a double saucepan. Flavour according to use and taste. Do not overheat or the fondant will lose its beautiful gloss and become brittle. Use it on all types of cakes as a covering or filling (mixed with butter) It will take many flavours, and can be used as a sweetmeat covered in chocolate.

Coconut Candy

Makes 675g/1½lb fondant   Preparation time: 25 minutes   Baking time: Nil

Using fondant as the base and coconut as the flavouring we can produce a simple sweet that goes well as one of an assortment of gift-wrapped homemade candies.

450g/1lb Fondant (page 178)
1 teaspoon gelatin
25ml/1fl oz water
275g/10oz coconut
Red colouring

Use a 30cm/12in square, 5cm/2in deep oiled metal tray

---

1   In a saucepan melt the fondant. Dissolve the gelatin in the water. Boil the fondant to 180°C/230°F. Add the coconut and the gelatin mix and stir well.

---

2   Pour half the hot sugar/coconut mixture onto the oiled tray. Allow to level and cool. In the remaining sugar, stir the red colouring and pour over the set white candy. Allow to cool before cutting into small squares. Store in a plastic bag or airtight container where it will keep for months.

Serving suggestion: Serve in paper cases and gift wrap. This is a much cheaper way of giving sweets than buying them from a shop. Also dip some squares into melted chocolate as an alternative.

Freezing: Does not freeze well but keeps in an airtight container for up to 3 months.

Buttercream

Makes 675g/1½lb   Preparation time: 15 minutes   Baking time: Nil

A light creamy base for all cakes, gateaux, etc., as a topping or filling. This mixture will pipe and produce many designs.

175g/6oz butter or margarine
450g/1lb icing sugar

50g/2oz evaporated milk
Vanilla essence

1 In a mixing bowl cream the butter, sugar, milk and vanilla essence to a light consistency. Scrape the sides and beat again for 5 minutes. Transfer to an airtight container

To Use: Flavour to suit the cake. Add melted chocolate to the buttercream for a really delicious filling and flavour with rum. To lighten the filling add egg whites. To make a fondant cream use half butter and half fondant and cream lightly.

Lemon Cheese

Makes 900g/2lb   Preparation time: 35 minutes   Baking time: Nil

This is a mixture of sugar and butter thickened with eggs. The flavour of fresh lemons makes this preserve a real treat on bread, scones or in cakes, flans or tarts. Will make a delightful filling for lemon meringue pies.

4 lemons
450g/1lb granulated sugar
175g/6oz butter
4 eggs or 10 yolks

1   In a saucepan boil the rind and juice of the lemons. Sieve and keep the juice. In a saucepan combine the sugar, butter, eggs and lemon juice and commence to heat slowly, stirring all the time until the curd begins to thicken. Adjust the flavour to taste. Proceed to bottle as for apricot purée. Lemon cheese will only keep for a few weeks so make only what you need.

To Use: Use for filling sponges, gateaux, pies, flans, tarts or as a sauce for steam puddings and ice cream desserts. Other fruits, namely blackcurrants, oranges, apples, or even bananas and tropical fruits, can be used to make your favourite fruit cheese.

Apricot Purée

Makes 850ml/1½ pints   Preparation time: 25 minutes   Baking time: Nil

Apricot purée is an ideal medium for glazing the tops of cakes, flans, Danish pastries, etc. Apart from the flavour, it keeps the base fresh and moist.

450g/1lb granulated sugar
450g/1lb apricot pulp, dried or
 fresh
75ml/3fl oz water

---

1   In a saucepan, stir the sugar, apricot pulp and water and then bring to the boil. Simmer slowly for 20 minutes until the temperature reaches 105°C/220°F. Sieve the jam and pour into sterilised warm jars. Fill to the brim and cover with waxed paper discs. Cool and cover with dampened cling film. Store in a dry dark place until required.

To Use: For all glazing, boil the purée/jam. Apply whilst hot. Other fruit jams can be made using the same principle. Allow extra pectin for those fruits which are low in this setting agent (i.e. strawberries and lemon) to compensate. Keeps for several weeks.

Sugar Syrup

Makes 850ml/1½ pints   Preparation time: 10 minutes   Baking time: Nil

A sugar syrup has many uses including the bottling of fresh fruit, softening fondant and making sweets and candies. It can also be used as a glaze for pastry and buns and will soften sponges in trifles and rum babas.

450g/1lb granulated sugar
400ml/14fl oz water

1   In a saucepan, dissolve the sugar in the water and boil the syrup for 2 minutes removing any surface material that may appear. Remove from the heat, strain and store in a jar till required.

2   Add mixed spice and lemon zest for glazing tea breads. For rum babas, boil the syrup and add rum and zest of lemon or orange. Soak the sponge whilst the liquid is still hot.

Rulenski Cheesecake

Makes 1   Preparation time: 25 minutes   Baking time: Nil

This recipe requires no baking. The creamy cheese filling marries well with the fresh strawberries for a really refreshing dessert.

For the base:
50g/2oz butter, melted
100g/4oz digestive biscuits
25g/1oz sesame seeds

For the filling:
225g/8oz cream or curd cheese
50g/2oz lemon curd

25g/1oz sugar
Zest and juice of a lemon
25g/1oz gelatin
50ml/2fl oz hot water
175g/6oz whipped cream
50g/2oz sultanas (pre-soaked in rum)
100g/4oz fresh strawberries

Use a 20cm/8in diameter, 5cm/2in deep cake hoop on a baking sheet/plate, oiled and with the edges lined with greaseproof paper.

1   For the base, melt the butter and mix in the sieved digestive biscuits and sesame seeds. Press mixture into the cake hoop and leave to set.

2   Blend together the cheese, lemon curd, sugar and the zest and juice of the lemon. Dissolve the gelatin in the hot water and add the whipped cream and sultanas. Scrape around the edges and mix to a smooth creamy filling. Pour onto the biscuit base and allow to set in the fridge. Remove cake hoop when set.

3   Cut the strawberries in half and arrange on top covering all the cheesecake. Cut and serve.

Variations: Use any fresh fruit in season. As an alternative to cream, use natural yoghurt and chop the fruit into cubes. Add to the cheese mixture. Finish with a sprinkling of toasted nuts or sesame seeds.

Serving suggestion: Serve as a dessert, straight from the fridge.

Freezing: Will freeze for up to 3 months or keep for 5 days in the fridge.

Windsor Mincemeat

Makes 900g/2lb   Preparation time: 25 minutes   Baking time: Nil

We all know that mincemeat is used in the festive mince pie but have you ever thought of making your own? Its easy, since all you need is a bowl and the ingredients — no cooking is required.

100g/4oz shredded suet or
  wholemeal breadcrumbs
100g/4oz dark brown sugar
100g/4oz seedless raisins
75g/3oz sultanas
150g/5oz currants
75g/3oz orange peel, minced
150g/5oz apples, peeled, chopped
  and cored
50g/2oz dates, stoned and
  chopped
25g/1oz lemon peel, chopped
25g/1oz mixed spice
Pinch of salt
Pinch of nutmeg
Zest and juice of an orange or
  lemon
76ml/3fl oz rum
25ml/1fl oz brandy
Stock syrup to bind

1   In a large bowl combine all the ingredients well. Leave in the bowl for 2—3 days. Pot the mincemeat into jars as for jam. Use when required. This will keep for several weeks stored in a dry cool place.

To Use: Use for filling pies, flans, tarts, or for steam puddings. Add other fruits, namely apricots, oranges or glacé cherries, for a different taste. Try adding almonds, hazelnuts, or walnuts which have been chopped.

Apple and Apricot Charlotte

Makes 1   Preparation time: 45 minutes   Baking time: 45 minutes

A healthy way to enjoy a dessert using fresh Irish Bramleys, apricots and slices of wholemeal bread baked in a Charlotte mould. A majestic pudding.

For the crust:
1 large wholemeal or white loaf, sliced
175g/6oz butter, melted

For the filling:
1.5kg/3lb apples, peeled, cored and sliced
75g/3oz apricot jam

75g/3oz demerara sugar
100g/4oz butter
100g/4oz raisins
75g/3oz dried apricots, chopped and soaked
Zest and juice of a lemon
2 cloves
Pinch of mixed spice
1 tablespoon rum

Use a Charlotte mould (2 litres/4 pints), well oiled

Pre-heat the oven to 200°C/400°F/Gas Mark 6
Microwave: 10 minutes.

---

1   Cut the slices of bread into long triangles so as to fit the mould. Dip into melted butter and arrange around the base and sides. The mould should be completely lined.

---

2   Cook together the apples, jam, sugar, and butter. When cooked, add the raisins, apricots, lemon, cloves, spices and rum. Mix thoroughly.

---

3   Pour the apple mixture into the mould to the top. Cover with the remainder of the bread and bake for 45 minutes until golden brown.

---

4   When baked, turn out on to a plate and serve hot.

Variations: *Summer Pudding:* Use raspberries, strawberries, loganberries or redcurrants.
Autumn Pudding: Again use blackberries, blackcurrants, bilberries or a mixture plus apples to give a better texture.

Serving suggestion: Serve hot or cold as a dessert with a fruit sauce, a whirl of fresh cream or yoghurt to complete a very wholesome sweet.

Freezing: Freezes for up to 3 months or refrigerates for 5 days.

Glossary

Absorb To take in; soaking of one substance into another

Aerate To incorporate air by mechanical or chemical means

Albumen A protein, such as egg white, used in meringues, mousses, etc

Ascorbic Acid Vitamin C, used as an improver in breadmaking, eliminating bulk fermentation

Bain Marie A double boiler — the French term for a large pot of hot water in which is placed a smaller pot, to avoid direct heat

Bakehouse The bakery where bread and confectionery is produced and baked

Bannock A large round bread scone or biscuit

Bap Morning roll, usually a soft dough rolled out flat and baked in a hot oven

Barm A yeast compound used as a leaven for bread, the forerunner to fresh baker's yeast

Barm Brack A flat fruit tea cake

Batch A selection of goods baked at the same time

Batter A liquid mixture of flour, egg, milk or water used for pancakes or coating prior to deep or shallow frying

Beat To introduce air by way of beating; whisking to make fluffy and light

Bind To hold together using eggs or similar liquid

Blanch To quickly immerse into hot water or oven in order to loosen skins (eg blanched almonds)

Blend The mixture of ingredients combined together to produce the required texture

Blind To bake blind prior to filling. Also refers to blind appearance on cakes or pikelets where the desired effect has not been attained. To bake blind a pastry case means to bake it alone before adding the filling and baking the whole together

Bloom Surface of breads and cakes. The word 'bloomer' referring to a loaf refers to overall appearance

Bridie A Scottish savoury-filled turnover (eg Forfar Bridie)

Chill To bring down to a temperature to just above freezing

Clear To 'clear' the batter or dough means beating it to a smooth, even consistency

Compote A mixture of fresh and dried fruits in a syrup served as a dessert

Compressed Yeast Manufactured fresh yeast in block form used commercially by bakers. Being alive, it acts quickly in a fermenting dough

Cottage Loaf A traditional loaf with two pieces of dough, one on top of the other This can be plain or notched to produce a crusty finish

Curdle When a liquid curdles the solids separate. This is caused by the addition of an acid or is due to beating

Custard A milk thickened with eggs or cornflour, and brought to the boil over a bain marie until thick

Dough A combination of flour, water or milk, salt and yeast kneaded into an elastic shape, usually for breadmaking

Dredge To sprinkle evenly over the surface with flour, sugar or any other powder

Dunking Dipping doughnuts or biscuits into coffee or hot chocolate

Farl A flat round quadrant-shaped bread made with wholemeal flour or oatmeal

Final Proof The last operation of breadmaking. The dough is allowed to rise before baking

Flan An open tart. The pastry is baked blind and various fruits and fillings are then added

Frangipane A sweet, rich filling for pastry cases made with butter, eggs, sugar and ground almonds

Freeze To solidify food for storage by lowering the temperature to below 0°C/32°F

Genoese A good quality cake used mainly for fondant fancies and gateaux

Girdle A type of griddle used in Scotland for baking scones and pancakes

Glacé Iced or glossy in appearance

Glaze To impart a shiny surface using eggs, gelatin, sugar, etc.

Griddle A circular iron pan on which scones, oatcakes and pancakes are baked

Handing Up A process whereby the dough pieces are moulded into balls before final proof

Infusion To immerse ingredients into a liquid to extract flavour

Knead The working of the dough by vigorous manipulation which strengthens the structure for final baking

Knockback To expel all the air from a risen dough before shaping

Kougelof A rich fermented bread similar to a savarin, baked in a mould and dredged with icing sugar

Pastry A stiff paste made with flour, fat, water or milk as a base for many confections, sweet or savoury

Pie A pastry case containing sweet or savoury fillings

Pinning The use of a rolling pin to flatten and sheet pastry or dough

Plait Three or more strands woven together

Preserve A way to store food by heat-treating or other methods

Prove The degree of aeration imparted by the action of the yeast on the dough

Purée A smooth, sieved pulp

Ripe Dough A term used to define the maturity of the fermented dough

Savoy Bag A triangular bag used for piping icing, creams, etc

Sheen In bread the cut surface; crumb appearance; the sparkle of the cells

Shortness The opposite of elasticity—in baking this means brittleness of pastry

Syrup A sugar/water mixture used for glazing and reducing icings

Steep To soak in water to extract soluble substances

Sugar Batter Method A process for making cakes in which the fats and sugars are creamed lightly and eggs added in stages. The flour is blended in with any liquid

Turnover A disc of pastry in the centre of which jam, mincemeat or fruit is placed The edges are moistened and folded over to form a semi-circular pastry

Unleavened Bread A dough consistency with no yeast added. This was the first type of bread made, before the introduction of fresh yeast

Whip To incorporate air into a mixture by beating the ingredients until light

Whisk Using a wire whisk to beat the ingredients to a light consistency (eg for sponges)

Wholemeal Flour made with 100% of the grain, ground either by roller mills or stone ground

Wheatmeal Flour which is milled to produce 85—90% of the grain

Wheat Germ The embryo of the wheat berry — very nutritious and rich in oils and vitamins

Yeast A pure culture, yeast is used to aerate all types of bread to produce a light-textured, well fermented bread loaf

Zest The layer of outer skin of citrus fruits used (grated) for flavour and as a garnish

Index